D1549671

The World of FOSSILS

SAMPSON LOW GUIDES

The World of FOSSILS

Vittorio De Zanche and Paolo Mietto

Sampson Low

Designers/Artists
Giorgio Arvati, Verona: 102 r; Luciano Corbella, Milan: 136, 189; Piero Cozzaglio, Brescia: 42, 46 l, 49, 52, 53, 54, 55, 71 b, 85 bl, 99 tl, 99 bl, 100 b, 109 b, 116–17, 120–1 b, 122, 123, 124, 129, 167, 169 t, 171, 173, 180, 184 t, 185, 187, 190, 191 l, 192 tr, 220 tl/tr, 224 t, 249; Di Ciancio, Milan: 121, 125 t; Raffaella Giacometti, Verona: 48, 51, 119, 178–9, 184 b, 188, 224 b, 225, 226, 227, 228 t, 229, 230, 231, 232, 234; Raffaello Segattini, Verona: 20, 43, 65, 66, 69, 72, 73 t, 80, 83 c, 91, 142, 192 b, 198, 238; Sergio, Milan: 246–7.

Photographs
The American Museum of Natural History, New York: 30, 115, 138, 139, 168, 182, 228 b; Archivio Mondadori, Milan: 9 tl, 10, 12, 44 (redrawn by Wenger), 47 (by kind permission of Prof. Hans Schaub), 60 t, 63 b, 64, 250, 251 l; Banca Popolare de Arzignano, Vicenza: 207 b; Carlo Bevilacqua, Milan: 200 b; British Museum, London: 73 b, 85 t, 87, 111 b, 124 b, 137 b, 164, 174–5, 183, 213, 239, 241 b; F. M. Carpenter: 221; Rodolfo Crespi, Milan: 16–17 b, 24 b, 201; Studio F & P, Verona: 7, 9 tr, 14, 16 t, 19, 26 b, 35, 46 r, 60 bl, 70, 95 b, 97, 103 r, 110, 112 t, 112 bl, 113, 126–7, 128, 146 b, 147, 148 tl, 148 b, 151 l, 153, 157, 160–1, 163 b, 169 b, 195 r, 203, 212 t, 214, 215, 217 b, 218, 222; Mario De Biasi: 172; M. Gaetani: 63 t, 156 b; H. Ibbeken: 21, 26 t, 36 t, 61, 62 b, 96 l, 101, 103 l, 105, 134, 143, 149 t, 151 r, 158, 159; Institute of Geological Sciences, published by permission of the Director, N.E.R.C. ©, Edinburgh: 11; Jacana, Paris: 237; Hayon: 251 r; G. Krampitz: 83 b; G. Leonardi/G. Pinna, Milan: 9 b, 15, 24 t, 25 t, 36 b, 37, 62 t, 67, 71 tl, 85 br, 100 t, 107, 109 t, 112 br, 120 l, 133, 135 r, 141, 145 t, 148 tr, 150, 152 b, 192 tl, 195 l, 202 r, 204, 209, 212 b, 244; Ligabue, Venice: 194; J.-L. Lubrano, Paris: 41; Arborio Mella, Milan: 240; Walter Mori: 199; G. Motto: 90 (coll. Campodonico), 96 r (coll. Campodonico); Musée Recontre/De Seynes, Paris: 162; Museo Civico di Storia Naturale, Verona: 220 b; Stuttgart Museum: 29; Museum Hauff, Holzmaden-Teck, Würtemberg: 31, 163 t; U.S. National Museum, Washington: 28 t, 79, 99 r, 106, 165; Naturhistorisches Museum, Vienna: 84; Mauro Pucciarelli: 95 t; Luisa Ricciarini, Milan: Archive B: 32 t, 71 tr, 76, 77 t, 89, 93, 98, 104–5, 111 t, 144, 145 b, 149 b, 152 t, 154, 155, 191 r, 202 l, 205, 206 b, 208 r; Carlo Bevilacqua: 23, 27, 32 b, 56–7, 94, 132, 137 t, 156 t, 206 t; Enrico Robba: 135 l, 200 t. Hans Rieber: 166; Royal Ontario Museum, Toronto: 77 b; Guido Ruggieri, Venice: 28 b, 33, 59, 60 br, 75, 146 t, 197; A. Scarnati: 242–3; J. W. Schopf: 83 t; Smithsonian Institution, Washington: 176–7; Stanghellini, Verona: 219; Studio IANTRA, Verona: 207 t, 210, 216, 217 t, 235, 241 t, 245; Université Pierre et Marie Curie, Paris: 81, 82; Luciano Vanzo, Verona: 3, 8, 208 l, 211.

The publishers would like to thank the following for providing specimens for photography: Museo Civico di Storia Naturale, Milan; Museo Civico di Storia Naturale, Verona; Museo dei Frati Francescani della Pieve di Chiampo, Vicenza. ;

Published in 1979 by
Sampson Low
Berkshire House, Queen Street,
Maidenhead, Berkshire SL6 1NF

SBN 562 00120 4

Printed in Italy

Contents

Introduction

Planet Earth was probably formed about 4,600 million years ago. Some 3,500 million years ago the first organisms appeared, and life began the long, exciting adventure that is still going on. Over the course of these many millions of years complex organisms have slowly evolved from the simple unicellular forms. The whole timescale of evolution is bewildering; the first known land plants, for example, are about 400 million years old, and the early amphibians appeared about 300 million years ago. Mammals emerged not later than 200 million years ago, while birds first appeared 150 million years ago. The human race is a comparative newcomer with a history of at least two million years.

We know this fascinating history of life and the history of Man because we have been able to unlock the secrets of the past. Physical and chemical processes have preserved the remains of the plant and animal organisms that once lived in the sea, on land and in the air, within sedimentary rocks – as fossils.

The secrets of past life lie buried in the ground, but excavations gradually bring them to light. It is a science in its own right, and the study of fossils has its own name – palaeontology. By applying strict scientific principles to the examination of fossils and by using our knowledge of living plants and animals it is possible to attempt to reconstruct the history of life.

What is a fossil?

It will never be possible to work out, even roughly, how many organisms have existed on Earth since life began, as only a tiny proportion has been preserved in the rocks as fossils.

Fossilization by its very nature is an exceptional event since the particular conditions that allow organic remains of animals and plants to be preserved occur only in a very few cases. In fact, it is far commoner for chemical, physical or biological processes to destroy completely, dead animals and plants, and leave no trace of their existence.

The remains of an organism that normally fossilize are the hard parts, for example shell or bone. The soft tissues usually decay, so that it is only in exceptional cases that these, or entirely soft-bodied organisms are preserved. Evidence of an animal's activity, such as tracks or burrows, are uncommonly preserved in the rocks; these are known as trace fossils.

A great deal of valuable information can be obtained from these remains. It is possible, for instance, to tell which particular group of organisms (living or extinct) the fossil animal or plant belonged to, and if the state of preservation is good, it is even possible to go on to work out its genus and species using zoological and botanical methods.

▼Casts of fossil shells (*Neomegalodon gumbeli*) from Triassic Alpine rock

▲ Bee preserved in Oligocene amber from the Baltic

▲ *Neuropteris gigantea,* a Carboniferous pteridosperm

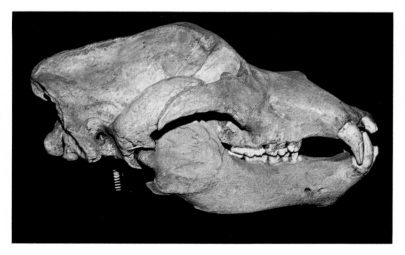

▲ Skull of cave bear (*Ursus spelaeus*)

9

▲ Impression of a reptile footprint in the Triassic rocks of Massachusetts

It is also possible to attempt to reconstruct the whole organism; we can try to find out about its direct or distant ancestors and its descendants; we can obtain information about the habitat in which it lived, where it died, and possibly the causes that led to its death. From the enclosing rocks it is possible to suggest the environment in which the organism lived, and the former geographical conformation of the area in which it was discovered. Fossils can also be used to date the rocks in which they occur.

Palaeontological evidence
The basic details of how life has evolved have been worked out; it is known that early forms of life were extremely simple, and that in the course of hundreds of millions of years increasingly complex forms evolved from them. Interestingly, most of the evolutionary processes that produced the present groups of animals and plants have taken place in a relatively recent period of the Earth's history – probably in the last 600 million years. This period of time, during which life on Earth underwent rapid diversification, is known as the Phanerozoic Era (literally, 'obvious life').

Although the basic patterns of the evolution of life are well

Petrified forest: the woody tissue ▶
has been replaced by mineral substances

▼ *Eoplatax papilio* an Eocene fish from Bolca in Italy

known, we still lack knowledge of detailed relationships between the various groups. Even our knowledge of relationships within major groups, even the better known ones, is still very incomplete in some cases. Insects, for example, a group of organisms at the peak of its development, appeared at least as far back as the Devonian period, but examples of fossil insects are generally uncommon and the number of known species is likely to be only a very small proportion of the actual number which existed. The precise origin of insects is still a mystery.

The oldest fossil birds are from the late Jurassic period, about 150 million years ago. Only three specimens have been found, all three from Solenhofen in Bavaria, and belonging to the species *Archaeopteryx lithographica*. If their wings had not left any impressions in the extremely fine-grained limestone in which they are preserved, the fossils might well have been classified as reptiles (which were very common and were of worldwide distribution during the Jurassic period), because their skeleton was still reptile-like. This strongly suggests that birds evolved from reptiles. Birds from the succeeding Cretaceous period (135–165 million years ago) more closely resemble modern birds, but we have not discovered any specimens of the transitional stages between the primitive Jurassic birds and the more developed birds of the Cretaceous period.

There are many other examples, but insects and birds demonstrate an important aspect of fossilization, and one that has significant repercussions on palaeontological evidence from a quantitative viewpoint. The chances of an organism being preserved as a fossil depend on the kind of substance it is composed of, the environment in which it lived, and the circumstances that allow its remains to escape complete destruction. Because most birds and insects lived on land, it is not difficult to see that they would have a very slim chance of becoming fossils. The three *Archaeopteryx* specimens were preserved in fine marine deposits, so their thin remains must have been washed into the sea. Many of the known fossil insects are immersed in a fossilized resin known as amber (see illustration on page 9).

There are other groups of organisms, however, that have a much better chance of becoming fossils because of their composition and their habitat. This is the case, for example, with bivalves, brachiopods, foraminifers, and radiolarians. These animals lived in water, and possessed a mineralized shell or skeleton, and had a chance of being buried rapidly. In such cases we have a much more complete knowledge of the fossils, which can be found in large numbers in some rocks.

13

Fossils as rock formers

When an organism fossilizes, it becomes an integral part of the rock in which it is preserved. In fact organisms have played, and do play, an important part in the formation of some kinds of rocks and many rocks contain varying proportions of material of organic origin. In these cases we talk of the importance of fossils

▲ Oligocene colonial coral

as rock formers. This phenomenon of rock formation with fossils can be seen quite clearly by examining a slab of fossil-bearing rock, such as limestone (this is sometimes used in buildings and pavements).

Some organisms such as colonial corals, algae and bryozoans, build rocks actively. All these rock-builders produce impressive structures which may rise high above the surrounding sea bed. However, other organisms such as radiolarians, foraminifers, molluscs, brachiopods, echinoderms and some algae, help to form rocks passively as their remains steadily accumulate over the years on the sea bed.

Fossils do not just have a quantitative role in forming rocks,

▲ Slab of Silurian limestone with rhynchonellid brachiopods

however. They can also influence their chemical and mineralogical composition, sometimes to a very great extent. The accumulation of radiolarian skeletons or diatom shells, for example, will produce a fine-grained rock composed of silica, while large quantities of calcareous or aragonitic shells (molluscs and echinoderms for example) will produce calcareous rock.

15

▲ Calyces of the crinoid *Encrinus carnalli*, from the Middle Triassic

▼ Thin section of fossiliferous limestone with nummulites

Collecting and studying fossils

The chances of extracting fossils from a rock depend to a large extent on several factors: the structure, composition, and toughness of the rock on the one hand, and the nature, composition, and state of preservation of the fossils on the other.

Fossils are almost always extracted mechanically – with hammers, chisels, drills and so on, but in certain cases can be chemically extracted by dissolving the fossils out with acid. Techniques of extraction require a good deal of expertise and patience, and inexperience can result in irreparable damage. Once the fossil has been extracted, cleaned and if necessary reconstructed and strengthened, the real work of identification begins. Books are obviously an invaluable source of information, and there are many to choose from. The bibliography at the back of the book provides a shortlist of the most useful titles to start with. A visit to a museum can help to bring all the book-learning to life. Although it may be possible to make some kind of identification, proper classification is as a rule done by specialists working in laboratories with access to good bibliographical research facilities.

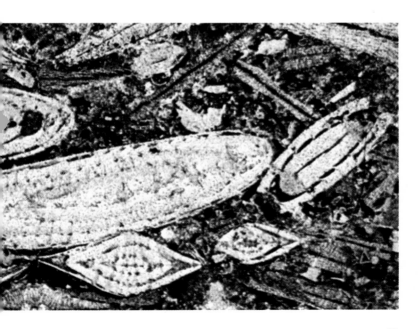

The Process of Fossilization

Fossilization is always an exceptional phenomenon, since the chemical and biological conditions that allow ancient plant and animal remains to survive occur very rarely. When an organism dies its soft parts decay or are eaten by scavengers. The hard parts survive, but rapid burial is necessary to ensure a chance of it being fossilized, when it will be protected from being broken up and destroyed. These conditions are more commonly met in the sea than on land. The conversion of soft sediments in which the remains are preserved – for example mud or sand – into rock is an important part of the fossilization process.

The processes involved are usually extremely slow, which

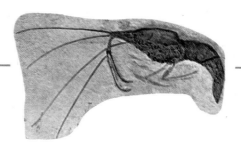

means that even if organic substances are buried rapidly, they might eventually still be destroyed, for example if the sediments are disturbed or rapidly eroded away.

The hard parts of organisms are composed of various substances. Calcium carbonate plays a particularly important role, and is commonly found in the form of calcite or aragonite in the shells and skeletons of invertebrate animals such as molluscs, corals, echinoderms, bryozoans, protozoans, and sponges and marine plants such as calcareous algae.

Other substances are also important, and some kinds of brachiopods, many arthropods and vertebrate bones in particular

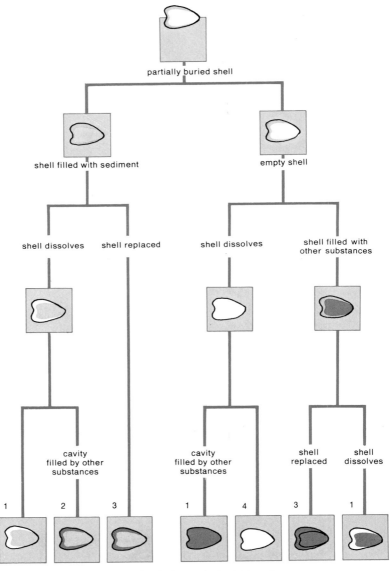

▲ Various modes of fossilization of a bivalve results in: 1. internal and external moulds; 2. replaced shell with internal and external moulds; 3. pseudomorphic shell with internal and external moulds; 4. natural cast

▲ External and internal moulds of a bivalve

contain phosphates. Chitin is found in many arthropods,
especially insects; silica in flagellates, diatoms, almost all
radiolarians and many sponges; and lignin is found in plants.

There are many methods of fossilization, some of them rather
complex. The most common are impregnation with mineral
solutions, encrustation, carbonization and solution. All are
connected in some way with the fomation of the enclosing rock.
This is particularly true of the first of these.

In the case of impregnation with mineral solutions, it is worth
looking at the process in some detail. Water percolates down
through the sediment as the temperature and pressure gradually
increase, and is largely responsible for the sediment turning into
rock. If there are no salts in the water the minerals forming the
skeleton of the organism lying in the sediment often dissolve
rapidly – which means no trace is left. When salts are present,
however, it is very different. In this case the minerals originally
present in the organism are impregnated or replaced by others
that are chemically more stable. Mineralized fossils are, in fact,
almost always composed of calcite or silica, sometimes of calcium
phosphate. In rarer instances they contain pyrite or iron oxide.
Other minerals are found only in extremely rare, practically
unique cases. These include sulphates of calcium, barium,
strontium and lead, silicates of iron and zinc, as well as
carbonates of zinc and copper.

There are many different ways in which the mineralized
substances contained in a shell or skeleton may be impregnated or
replaced, producing many different modes of preservation of a
fossil. For the sake of example, imagine a bivalve buried in
sediment. The following stages are the simplest, and the most

common, processes to which it could be subjected. The diagram on page 20 demonstrates the principles involved in graphic terms.

The negative image (known as the impression or external mould) of the external surface of the shell is imprinted on the sediment. The finer the sediment, the more perfect and detailed this impression will be. When the soft internal organs have decomposed and disappeared, the empty cavity that is left may be filled with the sediment surrounding the shell, or with other mineral substances. This produces an iternal mould or steinkern. The shell itself commonly dissolves and the void between the external and internal mould is filled with the mineral substances contained in the water percolating through the sediment. The original mineral substances comprising the shell can sometimes be replaced volume for volume by other minerals, which then faithfully reproduce even the tiniest details of the shell's original internal structure.

Suitably modified, the processes described above may be applied to a great many other groups of organisms, with only a few exceptions.

The practical importance of these various modes of preservation varies according to the group to which the fossil belongs. External moulds are sometimes more useful than internal moulds, and vice versa, while a combination of the two provides the most complete information. The internal mould of a lamellibranch, for example, will not be much use for identification purposes, since it carries no traces of shell ornamentation. But these marks do appear on the internal moulds of ammonites and nautiloids, together with traces of suture lines. The internal moulds of these organisms are therefore essential in identifying the various species.

What has been said so far obviously applies to organisms with internal cavities. A different process occurs with vertebrates. Their bones, which are mainly composed of organic substances, can become soft and spongy as certain of these decompose. The dissolved minerals percolating through the sediment may be deposited in the gaps that have been left, strengthening the bone remains and preserving their structure perfectly.

Under certain conditions ligneous substances also undergo a similar process, as in the case of the petrified tree trunks that faithfully preserve the interior structure of the original vegetable tissue. Examples of petrified trees can be seen in the picture on page 11, and a cross-section of a conifer trunk can be seen on the opposite page.

The process of encrustation has less connection with the

process of rock formation than the ones just described. In fact it occurs in relatively recent deposits, particularly on organisms that lived near, or were carried to, streams or waterfalls that were particularly rich in dissolved salts — especially calcium carbonate and silica. These salts may be deposited on an organism, which thus becomes encrusted with a thin mineral film. The organism is eventually destroyed, leaving behind a negative impression from

▲ Polished section of a Triassic conifer trunk replaced by silica

which it is possible to obtain a perfect cast using plaster or other substances. A classic example of this type of fossilization is provided by leaf impressions preserved in travertine.

As far as plants are concerned the most common process of fossilization is carbonization. It is connected with the action of anaerobic bacteria that remove the nitrogen, hydrogen and oxygen contained in plant matter, producing a relative

▲ *Mene rhombea*, a fish from the Eocene of Bolca, Italy

▲ Ammonite
preserved in pyrite

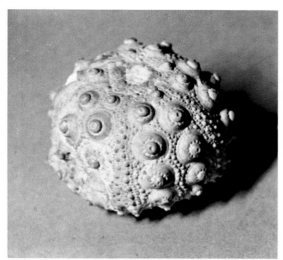

▲ *Hemicidaris*, a Jurassic echinoid

concentration of carbon. Coal was formed in this way, using up vast quantities of vegetable matter in the process. Studies of cell structure can often be carried out on carbonized plants, since even the most delicate structures can be preserved.

In some processes, the gases contained in the organic substance are removed without the direct intervention of bacteria. In this case a thin carbonaceous film is all that remains of the original organism.

It is clear that fossilization requires such a large number of favourable factors to be present that only very rarely does an organism become fossilized. It should also be remembered that many fossils may subsequently be destroyed by erosion of the rocks containing them, and that in the course of geological time the rocks of the Earth's crust sometimes underwent such dramatic changes that any fossils they may have contained would have been completely destroyed.

Extraordinary fossils
There are some cases of fossilization that can only be described as remarkable. These are generally fossils whose soft parts have somehow managed to survive along with the hard parts. Apart from being undoubtedly dramatic these cases provide extremely

Fossil palm from the Eocene of Bolca, Italy ▶

▲ Mummified body of a prehistoric man

▼ Oligocene chelonian (*Tryonyx capellini*) from Monteviale in Italy

▲ *Aysheaia pedunculata*, Cambrian onychophoran from Burgess shale of British Columbia

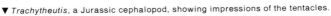

▼ *Trachytheutis*, a Jurassic cephalopod, showing impressions of the tentacles.

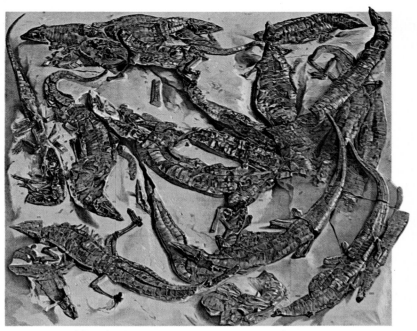

▲ Part of a slab containing Triassic thecodont reptiles
(*Aetosaurus*) (the complete slab contains 24 specimens)

useful indications of what the organisms must have looked like –
and sometimes such complete remains even make it possible to
deduce a considerable amount about the life habits of such
creatures.

Fossils with such detail generally come from a certain kind of
fossil-bearing bed, where they are common. These rocks are
formed from extremely fine-grained sediments, and the organic
remains being deposited during the sedimentation process were
buried very quickly. Sometimes there are enormous numbers of
organic remains, and some deposits containing them are called
'fossil graveyards', possibly representing areas into which
organisms strayed accidentally, became trapped and met a
sudden death. Perhaps a more likely, though less dramatic,
explanation may be that concentrations built up in certain areas
because of ocean currents. A good example is a slab of Triassic
sandstone that was found at Würtemberg. In an area two metres
square some 24 specimens of the reptile *Aetosaurus* were found.

An extremely fine-grained original sediment is usually a basic condition for the preservation of some very delicate structures. One of the most well-known examples of this is the Solenhofen limestone in Bavaria. The very fine-grained rocks of this area have yielded some extremely beautiful specimens belonging to various groups of animals, including insects with distinct wing impressions, cephalopods with tentacles and their ink sac still full of colouring matter, impressions of jellyfish, flying reptiles (pterosaurs) with impressions of their membraneous wings, and many other intersting fossils. The most famous fossils from Solenhofen are the three specimens of the fossil bird *Archaeopteryx lithographica*, which are complete with perfect wing impressions.

The early Jurassic limestone of Holzmaden (Würtemberg) has yielded many specimens of ichthyosaurs (dolphin-like marine reptiles), clearly showing the outline of the body as well as the skeleton. Many of the females have foetuses in their womb, and

▼ Eggs of the Cretaceous dinosaur *Protoceratops*

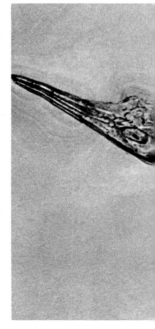

one female died apparently in the act of giving birth (this can be seen in the photograph reproduced below). These finds are extremely important, allowing us to examine interesting biological aspects of these extinct animals.

Shales of Cambrian age from Burgess Pass in British Columbia have produced a large number of beautifully preserved invertebrate fossils, including soft-bodied 'worms', trilobites complete with limbs, and many strange arthropods, preserved as flattened films in the fine-grained rocks. The Eocene limestone of the famous deposit at Bolca in Italy has yielded insects, bird feathers and flowers, as well as magnificent specimens of fish showing the outline of the body. The Oligocene deposits of the Baltic in particular have produced perfectly preserved flowers and insects completely immersed in amber (fossilized pine resin). A good example is shown on page 9.

The American Cretaceous rocks have yielded two mummified specimens of the reptile *Anatosaurus*, with fragments of skin

▼ An *Ichthyosaurus crassicostatus* that died giving birth (several foetuses can be seen under the ribs, and there is a new-born specimen on the right)

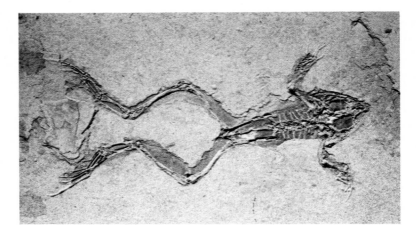

▲ *Rana pueyoi*, a Miocene frog

preserved. The nearly perfectly preserved mammoth and rhinoceros remains that were 'deep-frozen' in the ice of Siberia are even more spectacular, and finally at Quercy in France, phosphatized bats, frogs and snakes have been found.

There are many cases where original colour has been preserved, especially in shells of molluscs dating from the end of the Cainozoic Era. Such cases are uncommon in pre-Cretaceous deposits, although there are instances of Devonian and Permian

◀ *Natica tigrina*, a Pleistocene gastropod, showing traces of original colouring

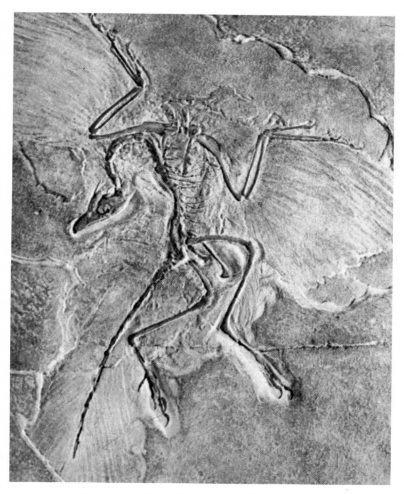

▲ *Archaeopteryx lithographica*, a Jurassic bird,
showing distinct wing impressions

brachiopods carrying traces of original colour.

Some fossils are extraordinary for other reasons, as for
example the nests of Cretaceous dinosaur eggs found in Mongolia
or the fossilized evidence of the diseases that some organisms
suffered from when they were alive.

Geological Time

The scale of geological time is too vast to appreciate in everyday terms. The scientific breakthrough that has enabled us to measure its extent accurately did not come until the beginning of the twentieth century, when radioactivity was discovered. Before this geologists had to estimate time by calculating how long layers of rock took to accumulate, and the results turned out to be a gross underestimation.

Nevertheless there was great interest in finding out the true extent of geological time even before radioactive dating, and it had been stimulated by Charles Darwin's theories about evolution during the last century. Scientists tried to find out how long

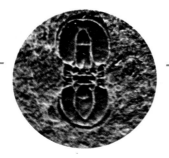

the world had existed in many ways, including experiments based on the salinity of the sea and the thickness of sedimentary rocks.

In the first case they started from the premise that sea water was originally fresh and that salinity was a property acquired as time went by. By calculating the increase in the salinity after a certain number of years, it would according to them be possible to work out when the first water on Earth had condensed. However the results produced a figure that was far lower than the real extent of geological time. In the second case it was supposed that the thickness of sedimentary rocks was proportional to the duration of time, so once it was known how fast various types of rock

sedimented the length of geological time could be calculated. This experiment did not give the desired results either, because the speed of sedimentation is too variable, and in any case rock strata contain too many undocumented periods of time, or stratigraphic gaps as scientists term them.

▼ Slab of Silurian shale with graptolites

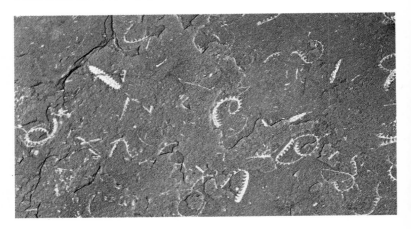

▲ The early Jurassic ammonite *Dactylioceras tenuicostatum*

Radioactive dating

To measure geological time scientists had to find something that was not influenced by other variables except time itself – in other words a phenomenon that occurred independently of the environment, especially temperature and pressure. The decay of radioactive elements into other stable or more stable elements was the perfect answer, and the first measurements, though still inaccurate, produced results that were more in line with the real extent of geological time.

Radioactive dating depends upon the rate of decay of radioactive isotopes of elements; those most commonly used for dating rocks are uranium, potassium-argon, rubidium-strontium and carbon 14. The dating method is based on the fact that in a certain time (which differs according to the element), half a radioactive element decays; this is called the half-life. In rocks containing such elements it is possible to work out how much of the element has decayed, and thus how long the process of decay has been occurring. The half-lives of some radioactive elements range up to thousands of millions of years, thus allowing the very oldest rocks to be dated. There can be a fairly large margin of error with radioactive dating, especially with very ancient rocks.

Not all rocks contain radioactive elements, but those which do can be used to provide convenient datum lines from which it is possible to estimate the age of the other intervening rocks.

Relative chronology

Another method of dating is known as relative chronology. It involves putting various events, both physical and biological, that have occurred throughout geological time into the correct chronological order.

Relative chronology is essentially based on two principles. The first principle is to put phenomena in sequence according to when they happened in relationship to one another. For example sequences of rock strata, each layer is more recent than the one beneath, and at the same time older than the one above. This is a universal law. Nevertheless this sequence is sometimes reversed in regions such as mountain ranges where the rocks have been intensely folded. Whole strata may be upturned, and in the case of folded rock strata it will be clear that these have been laid down before folding occurred.

The second principle is that every period of geological time (at least in Phanerozoic times) may be identified by unique and distinctive fossil 'assemblages'. In other words we can say that rock strata containing the same fossils are the same age, and were formed at the same time. In this way it is also possible to correlate rocks of areas distant from one another. Nevertheless, much care is needed with fossil correlations, because appearances can be deceptive. Two groups of strata containing the same fossils may not always be the same age; individuals of the same species may have migrated and so may appear in different places at different times, although the time scales involved in such cases are small.

Another reason why identical fossil assemblages do not always indicate contemporaneity between two groups of strata may be because the fossils in one of the two areas have been eroded out of their original rocks and rearranged – in other words, redeposited in more recent sediment.

Relative chronology therefore simply tells us the order in which events happened, without giving us any indication about how long ago they took place. Sequences worked out on the basis of relative and absolute chronology can usefully be used side by side to measure geological time.

Geologists have divided the history of the Earth into several major chapters known as eras. These are subdivided further into periods, epochs and ages. The lines separating these periods from each other commonly correspond to important geological and palaeontological events, such as the formation of mountain chains or the appearance or extinction of certain groups or species of organisms. These major periods of geological time are set out in the table on page 39, which also shows the relative duration of the eras.

ERA	PERIOD	YEARS AGO (millions)	DURATION (in millions of years)
(Quaternary)	HOLOCENE	0.008	
(Quaternary)	PLEISTOCENE		
		1.5–2	
CAINOZOIC (Tertiary)	PLIOCENE		5.5
CAINOZOIC (Tertiary)		7	
CAINOZOIC (Tertiary)	MIOCENE		19
CAINOZOIC (Tertiary)		26	
CAINOZOIC (Tertiary)	OLIGOCENE		12
CAINOZOIC (Tertiary)		38	
CAINOZOIC (Tertiary)	EOCENE		16
CAINOZOIC (Tertiary)		54	
CAINOZOIC (Tertiary)	PALAEOCENE		11
		67	
MESOZOIC	CRETACEOUS		70
MESOZOIC		135	
MESOZOIC	JURASSIC		55
MESOZOIC		190	
MESOZOIC	TRIASSIC		35
		225	
PALAEOZOIC	PERMIAN		55
PALAEOZOIC		280	
PALAEOZOIC	CARBONIFEROUS		65
PALAEOZOIC		345	
PALAEOZOIC	DEVONIAN		50
PALAEOZOIC		395	
PALAEOZOIC	SILURIAN		45
PALAEOZOIC		440	
PALAEOZOIC	ORDOVICIAN		60
PALAEOZOIC		500	
PALAEOZOIC	CAMBRIAN		70
		570	
PRECAMBRIAN			4,000
PRECAMBRIAN		4,600	

RELATIVE DURATION OF ERAS

CAINOZOIC
MESOZOIC
PALAEOZOIC
PRECAMBRIAN

▲ Geological time scale

Evolution

When Jean-Baptiste Lamarck and Charles Darwin proposed their theories of evolution in 1809 and 1859 respectively, they met with blank incomprehension, the heritage of a mentality that implicitly believed in the scientific truth of the events described in the Bible. Many of the contemporary scientists, however eminent, were unable to grasp the deeper significance of evolution.

One such scientist was Georges Cuvier of the 'catastrophe theory'; he was one of the first scientists to use fossils as stratigraphic tools and he suggested that major catastrophes periodically struck the biological world, destroying it completely. However from time to time there would be periods of creation to regenerate

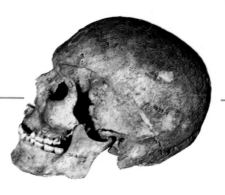

what had been destroyed. In this way he tried to explain the reason why some organisms disappeared and new forms emerged. Cuvier's ideas influenced the majority of contemporary scientists, including D'Orbigny who established 27 periods to correspond with 27 'acts of creation', but they were finally demolished by the cast-iron proof that evolutionists found to support their theories.

In fact it is wrong to talk of a 'theory' of evolution any longer, since the concept of a biological world in constant evolution has been widely documented and is no longer questioned. Even the underlying causes of evolution have lost a great deal of their

EVOLUTION

mystery. Discoveries in different branches of biology have enabled us to establish that the basic processes regulating evolution are to found in genetic mutation and natural selection. Indeed, the basic principles of evolution are used by plant and animal breeders to produce breeds and strains adapted to suit our needs. Geneticists today are only speeding up and controlling what is fundamentally a natural process of evolution. In nature, it is a much more random situation than in the laboratory.

Evolution is such a slow process, however, that it is difficult to examine it in action. This partly explains why it took so long for this concept to be accepted and shows the importance of palaeontology which enables us to add the time dimension. The relationships between species, or those between different groups of organisms, can only be unravelled by studying fossils.

To look at the living biological world and compare it with fossil discoveries might give a distinct impression that evolution has progressed in sudden jerks. But careful examination of series of fossils collected from successive rock strata in the same area has shown that evolution is a continuing process, characterized by tiny variations at species level (the lowest unit into which animals and plants, fossilized and living, are classified). Between the higher units, such as genera, families and orders, there is commonly an apparent discontinuity, but these gaps may be

▼ Skeleton and reconstruction of the amphibian *Ichthyostega*

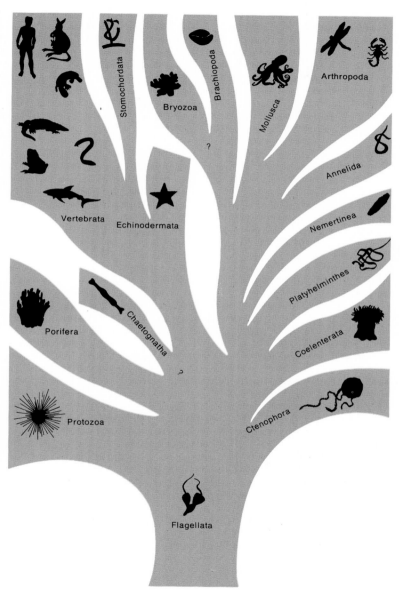

Stomochordata

Brachiopoda

Bryozoa

Mollusca

Arthropoda

?

Annelida

Vertebrata

Echinodermata

Nemertinea

Chaetognatha

Platyhelminthes

Porifera

Coelenterata

?

Protozoa

Ctenophora

Flagellata

▲ Evolutionary relationships in the Animal Kingdom

43

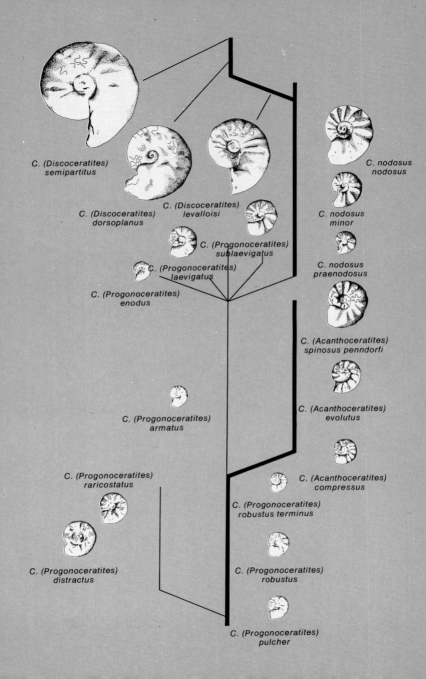

C. (Discoceratites)
semipartitus

C. (Discoceratites)
dorsoplanus

C. (Discoceratites)
levalloisi

C. (Progonoceratites)
sublaevigatus

C. (Progonoceratites)
laevigatus

C. (Progonoceratites)
enodus

C. nodosus
nodosus

C. nodosus
minor

C. nodosus
praenodosus

C. (Acanthoceratites)
spinosus penndorfi

C. (Acanthoceratites)
evolutus

C. (Progonoceratites)
armatus

C. (Acanthoceratites)
compressus

C. (Progonoceratites)
raricostatus

C. (Progonoceratites)
robustus terminus

C. (Progonoceratites)
distractus

C. (Progonoceratites)
robustus

C. (Progonoceratites)
pulcher

bridged by isolated discoveries. In the final analysis, however, all links in the evolutionary process are from one species to another. Over a long period of time the genetic branches that gradually develop become sufficiently diverse to be counted as different genera.

Evolution from species to species

It has already been stated that the species is the lowest unit with which palaeontologists or biologists normally work. Only a tiny proportion of organisms is ever fossilized with enough regularity and frequency to allow statistical studies and so enable us to appreciate the minimal variations that occur when one species evolves into another. Some of the easiest organisms on which to do this type of research are invertebrates (animals without backbones). The reason for this is that such animals tend to form the most abundant fossils. When one tries to work out and reconstruct the evolution of specific organisms at species level, special conditions are necessary for the investigations to have any validity. One of these, as has been said, is to have at one's disposal as many specimens as possible from successive beds in the same area, although rock strata are not always continuous, and there are commonly gaps in the sequence.

Organisms in one area may evolve from one species into another due to changing environmental conditions, as in the following example. The Pleistocene snail *Viviparus* from Slavonia evolved from smooth-shelled forms to forms with increasingly ornamented and complex shells. The cause of this change was very probably a local increase in the salinity (saltiness) of the water in which the snails lived.

Geographical or ecological isolation of two groups of the same species might result in each evolving into a new species. However, it is often practically impossible to establish which of the two isolation factors may have occurred.

It is natural to think that, of the two, geographical factors must have been much more important, but it is clear that very often ecological isolation was far more directly responsible for the evolutionary phenomenon of a new species.

A species developed by geographical isolation is illustrated by the ammonite-like cephalopod *Ceratites*, which inhabited the Mediterranean part of the Tethys basin during the Triassic period. It penetrated the Germanic basin through channels that temporarily linked the two basins at two different periods, and two different species evolved in the two basins. The evolution of the genus *Ceratites* is shown in graphic form in the diagram on the opposite page.

◀ Evolution of the Middle Triassic cephalopod genus *Ceratites*

The evolution of the Cretaceous sea-urchin *Micraster* provides an example of ecological isolation. There are different *Micraster* species all derived from the same parent coexisting within the same distribution area. Comparing them with living sea-urchins of a similar kind has shown that *Micraster* lived buried in the sediment of the sea bed and that individual species adapted to living at different depths. This meant that individual species occupied different ecological niches and so became isolated from each other.

Evolution in the major groups

As far as major groups of organisms are concerned, there is commonly very striking palaeontological evidence suggesting relationships between groups which apparently have nothing in common with one another.

Considered on this level, evolution seems even more extraordinary. Evolution of major groups nevertheless follows the same pattern as evolution from species to species. The evolution of one group of organisms into another must necessarily be reduced to the evolution of one species into another. A further

▼ Reconstruction of the early scorpion *Palaeophonus nuncius*

▼ Slab with specimens of the inarticulate brachiopod *Lingula*

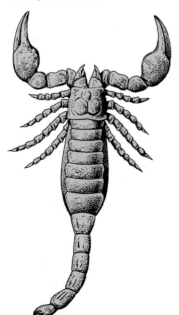

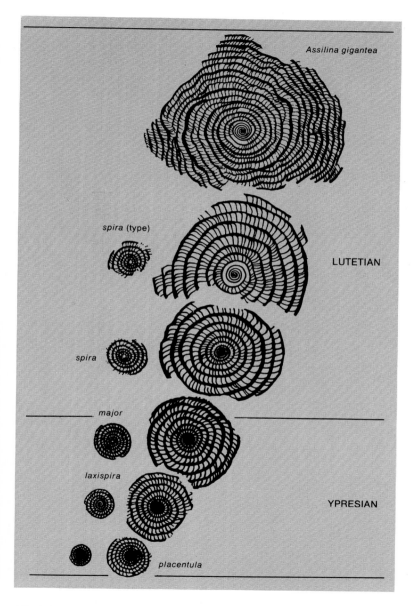

Assilina gigantea

spira (type)

LUTETIAN

spira

major

laxispira

YPRESIAN

placentula

▲ Evolution of the foraminifer *Assilina spira*

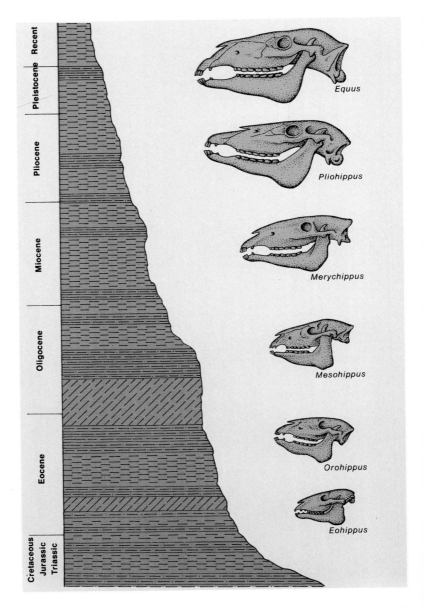

Evolution of the skull of a horse ▲

reason for this apparent discontinuity is that while the species is the basic biological unit, the higher groupings are often artificial ones that have been established according to very different principles.

The evolution of one group into another never occurs suddenly but as a result of tiny modifications affecting chronologically successive species that possess the combined characteristics of the two groups. Until the characteristics of one group eclipse those of another such species are known as transitional boundaries or, more popularly, 'missing links'.

The principle can be seen clearly with the primitive bird

▼ Evolution of amphibians

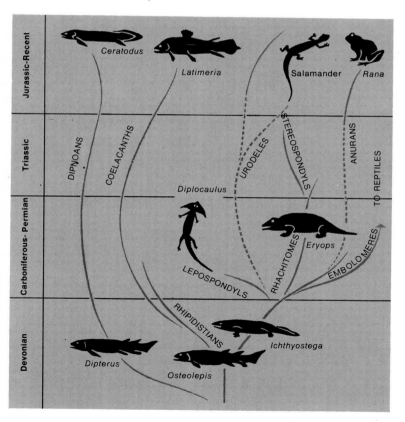

Archaeopteryx, mentioned earlier in this book. One can in fact speculate about it at length. This fossil contains both reptile and bird characteristics, the reptilian ones deriving from a group of dinosaurs called archosaurs. It is only because the *Archaeopteryx* specimens were fossilized in an extremely fine sediment that traces of wing impressions survived. These show that *Archaeopteryx* was a bird, although a bird with definite reptilian characteristics. If this extremely important feature had not been preserved, *Archaeopteryx* would probably have been regarded as a reptile and the origin of birds would have remained shrouded in mystery. Even now the problem has not been completely solved, for there is a gap between *Archaeopteryx* and the nearest archosaur, *Saltoposuchus*.

Scientists have tried to bridge this gap by 'inventing' the *Proavis*, a creature containing some of the characteristics of its archosaur ancestors and some belonging to primitive birds (so far *Archaeopteryx* is the only known representative of this last group). An artist's impression of what the '*Proavis*' could have looked like is on page 188, with a reconstruction of *Archaeopteryx lithographica* shown on page 189.

Evolution in the major groups also gives a distinct impression that it must have occurred suddenly, particularly among vertebrates. One of the main reasons for this is that the vertebrate fossil remains are much less common than those of invertebrates. The evolution of vertebrates is most often influenced by factors acting on small and highly specialized populations living in particular ecological niches that condition their pattern of evolution. This obviously makes it more difficult to find not only uninterrupted sequences in which evidence of evolution at species level has been preserved, but isolated finds as well. In fact the study of vertebrates and their evolution often has to be done with isolated finds from areas a long way apart from each other.

A really classic example of environmental influence on the evolution of vertebrates is offered by the horse family. In the evolutionary history of these mammals, we see the importance of mutation, isolation and natural selection, enabling horses gradually to adapt to a rapidly changing environment.

In the evolutionary history of the horse, a process that started in the Eocene, about 50 million years ago, there is at one extreme *Eohippus* (or *Hyracotherium*), a small quadruped that lived in forests, and at the other *Equus*, the modern horse that adapted to living on grassland. The gradual adaptation to its present habitat was accompanied by important anatomical changes. Starting with *Eohippus*, there was a gradual increase in size, together with dramatic modifications of the limbs, which change from four-toed to single-toed. The shape of the skull and especially the teeth also indicate that evolution was a smooth process (horses' teeth were first adapted to chewing leaves, but they gradually became better fitted to coping with a diet based on grass). One of the reasons for these changes can undoubtedly be found in the changes of climate

▼ Left: evolution of proboscidean skull
Right: upper molars of fossil proboscideans (view of crown)

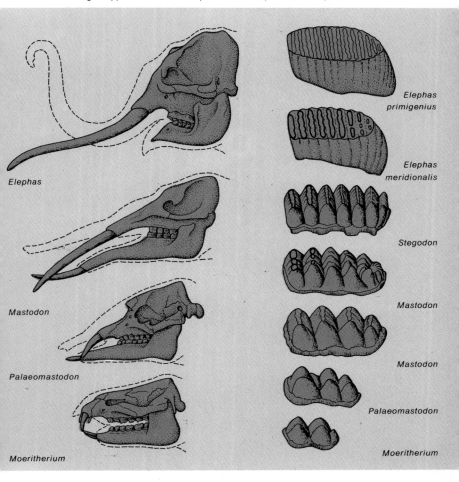

Elephas

Mastodon

Palaeomastodon

Moeritherium

Elephas
primigenius

Elephas
meridionalis

Stegodon

Mastodon

Mastodon

Palaeomastodon

Moeritherium

51

that occurred during the Cainozoic Era, producing vast plains where there had once been forests. Because horses had to be able to move quickly in these wide open spaces to escape from predators and because the new environment provided them with a different kind of diet, their way of life changed dramatically. So in the course of time they acquired the characteristics of the modern horse. The evolutionary development of the horse is clearly shown in the diagram on page 234. This is useful if read in conjunction with the drawings on page 48 showing the

▼ Evolution of sinapsid reptiles

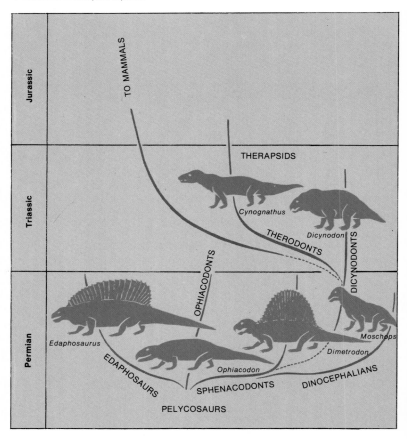

development of the skull of the horse from Eocene times to the present day.

There are many other groups of vertebrates that can be mentioned here, titanosaurs for example, mammals that lived during the Eocene and Oligocene periods and disappeared without leaving any descendants, and proboscideans. In spite of the large number of proboscidean finds, our knowledge of their evolutionary history, which began towards the end of the Eocene period, is still incomplete, and scientists only have a rough idea of how it developed. The greatest problem that is encountered in the study of proboscideans is the existence of parallel evolutionary lines whose interconnecting relationships have still to be completely worked out.

Although tracing the evolutionary path taken by these and other groups of creatures in the course of time is really fascinating, it is just as interesting to discover that many other

▼ Evolution of lepidosaurian and archosaurian reptiles

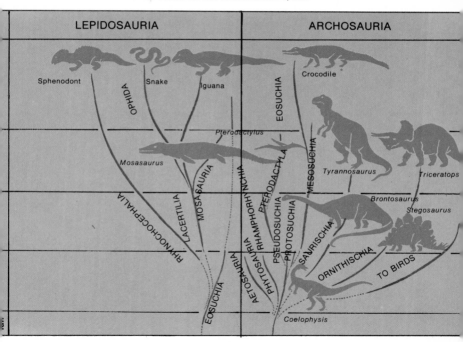

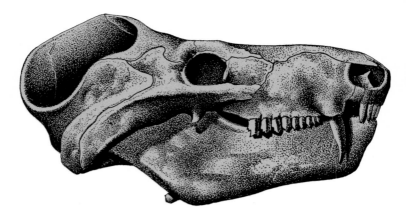

▲ Skull of the Triassic mammal-like reptile *Cynognathus*

groups stayed relatively unchanged throughout vast periods of time. Palaeontological evidence for this phenomenon is extensive. There are striking similarities between *Paleophonus nuncius* from the Silurian period (about 400 million years old), which is regarded as the first exclusively terrestrial animal, and the present-day scorpion; another example is *Lingula*, an inarticulate brachiopod that appeared during the Ordovician period, and which can still be found in the sea today (see page 46).

From these few examples it will be evident that there are no general rules governing the time organisms take to evolve. For some groups the time is very short; for others it takes hundreds of millions of years.

The history of animal evolution has many other surprising features, such as homoeomorphism and convergence. In these cases, species of entirely different origins can become extremely similar in appearance, or can take on a broadly similar form. Examples of convergence are found with richtofenids (Permian brachiopods) and rudists (Cretaceous bivalves) which grow in 'reefs' and each bears a strong resemblance to colonial corals, since they adopted a similar mode of life. A further example is afforded by the general similarity in form of ichthyosaurs (extinct marine reptiles) and dolphins (living marine mammals).

The story of evolution has come a long way since Lamarck and Darwin launched their theories on the world, and fossil records have played an important part in establishing the true relationships of genera and species over a period of time. One of the fascinations of fossil hunting is that there is always the remote possibility of another 'missing link' being discovered.

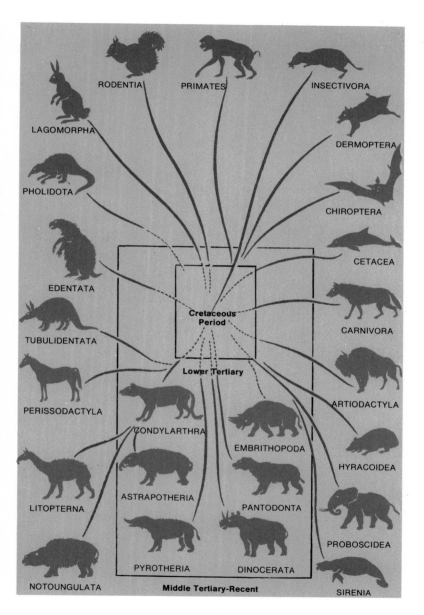

RODENTIA
PRIMATES
INSECTIVORA
LAGOMORPHA
DERMOPTERA
PHOLIDOTA
CHIROPTERA
EDENTATA
CETACEA
TUBULIDENTATA
CARNIVORA
PERISSODACTYLA
ARTIODACTYLA
CONDYLARTHRA
EMBRITHOPODA
LITOPTERNA
ASTRAPOTHERIA
HYRACOIDEA
PANTODONTA
PROBOSCIDEA
PYROTHERIA
DINOCERATA
NOTOUNGULATA
SIRENIA

Cretaceous Period

Lower Tertiary

Middle Tertiary–Recent

▲ Probable relationships between groups of fossil and living placental mammals   55

VI·E

▲ Fossilized skeleton of *Vomeropsis longispinus*

The Uses of Fossils

One of the first questions anyone interested in palaeontology will wish to ask, is what the extinct and primitive creatures were like. This is understandable as most fossils are only parts of organisms rather than complete ones. The most resistant parts are those which are generally preserved, while the 'soft' parts rapidly decayed. A snail, for example, leaves only its shell; a vertebrate leaves only bones, or sometimes just the teeth. The problem lies in building up a picture of what an organism looked like on the basis of such incomplete remains.

Some fossils provide sufficient evidence for us to get a pretty good idea of what an animal or plant might have looked like. The

shape, size and decoration of a bivalve shell, for example, can tell us exactly what its external appearance was. Inspection of the inside of the shell can reveal the position of the hinge line and the edge of the mantle, as well as the muscle scars. Comparison of these features and the general shape of the shell with those of modern bivalves can give a lot of information about the habits and mode of life of the bivalve which produced the fossil. It is possible to determine, for example, whether it lived attached to rocks, or if it burrowed in soft sediment.

Vertebrate fossils can be reconstructed in similar ways, and comparison with living animals can indicate from which part of

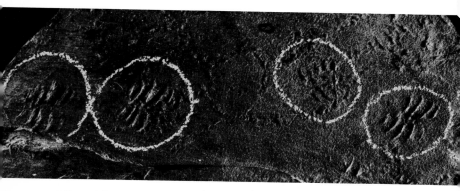

▲ Traces left on the sea bed by a straight-shelled nautiloid

the skeleton a particular bone comes. Even if there are only just a few bones available, it is sometimes possible to suggest what the entire skeleton might have looked like. Muscle attachment areas can lend a clue as to the strength and size of the original muscles, and the shape and size of the bones themselves can suggest, for example, if the animal was a slow mover or a fast runner. The teeth are vitally important in indicating the diet of an animal – herbivores and carnivores are each characterized by a particular type of dentition.

While it is often possible to get a general idea of the living organism from the fossils, there are details of soft parts which can

▼ Trilobite *Flexicalymene meeki*   ▼ Belemnite shell or 'guard' in section

 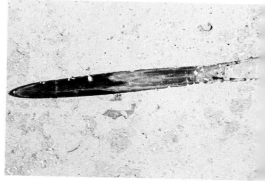

▲ Crinoids (*Bactrocrinites*) attached to the shell of a nautiloid (*Orthoceras*)

◄ Fossil excrement (coprolite)

▲ Impression of a gastropod trail
preserved in Eocene sandstone

never be found out – for example whether the animal was warm
or cold blooded. Some exceptionally well-preserved fossils can,
however, provide information about the soft parts, or can help
solve certain problems posed by the structure of the skeleton. In
the latter case, the ichthyosaur provides a good example. The
backbone of this Jurassic fish-like reptile bends sharply
downwards at the tail end. Examination of some of the first
ichthyosaurs to be discovered seemed to suggest that this was a
deformity, perhaps brought about by pressures exerted on the
skeleton after burial. However, all ichthyosaur skeletons
discovered subsequently were found to have the same 'deformity'.

▲ Bivalve fossilized in 'life position';
insert, living specimen

When a well-preserved specimen was found in which the outline
of the body was preserved around the skeleton, it was seen that
the downward bend of the back bone corresponded to the lower
lobe of the tail fin, while the upper lobe had no bone in it at all.

From the best-preserved fossils it is possible to find out much
more than just appearance. For example, some dinosaurs and
mammoths have been found with remains of food in the gut, a
female ichthyosaur has been found with foetuses still in the body,
and cave bears have been discovered with spinal deformities
caused by arthritis. Well-preserved bone or plant material can
even show details of the cell structure.

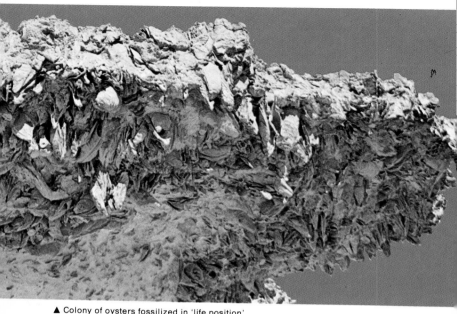
▲ Colony of oysters fossilized in 'life position'

Palaeobiologists usually have to rely on incomplete and often poor evidence because of the very nature of the material which they are working with, and it is the occurrence of the rare exceptionally-preserved fossils which has enabled them to gain detailed information about a handful of organisms. Nevertheless, careful and painstaking work on less complete material has allowed them to discover a remarkable amount about a large number of extinct organisms.

Palaeoecology

As well as studying individual fossils, and attempting to work out as much as possible about the organisms from which they are derived, the palaeobiologist will also want to find out how and where these organisms lived. The study of such relationships in living organisms is called ecology; this study applied to fossils is called palaeoecology. When dealing with living organisms, relationships between them and the environment can be observed at first hand. In palaeoecology these relationships have to be deduced by indirect means.

THE USES OF FOSSILS

There are a great many environments in the modern world.
They can broadly be divided into two sets, those in the sea and
those on land. In the sea the number of environments is much
smaller, and comprises those of the sea bed — littoral, bathyal,
abyssal — and those within the body of water itself, such as

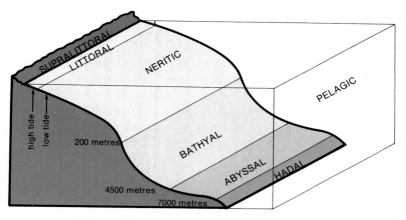

▲ Diagram of marine environments

neritic, oceanic, epipelagic and bathypelagic. These are all related
to depth and to distance from the shore; within each there are
variants depending, for example, upon kind of substrate (e.g.
sandy or rocky) or latitude.

On land different environments are more obvious, including
tundra, tropical rain forest, arid desert, grassland, temperate
deciduous forest, and so on. It must be remembered, however,
that each particular environment is unique in its own right — not
all temperate deciduous forests are the same, and various
biological, physical and chemical factors come into play, and all
these are important in ecological studies. Many are just not
available to the palaeoecologist — for example, temperature,
pressure, salinity, distance from the shore. While most ecological
studies have been made on terrestrial environments, the fossil
record naturally has a very heavy bias towards marine organisms,
so that in contrast palaeoecology tends to be restricted largely to
marine environments.

When associations of fossils are found in a layer of rock, it
must first be established whether they represent an original living

assemblage or whether the association is merely one which has been washed in by water currents from elsewhere. There are several ways of finding this out, both by detailed studies of the fossils themselves and from studying the sediments in which they are buried. It is not difficult to judge whether a fossil has been transported, or whether it is still in 'life position'. It is often useful to make comparisons with modern assemblages, just as it is for reconstructing the individual fossils themselves. Fossil coral reefs, for example, can readily be identified by comparison with their living counterparts, and this kind of comparison can yield a good deal of information about the past environment.

Palaeoecology is still in its early days, and doubtless the contribution it has to make will increase in the future.

Palaeoclimatology

Climate is undoubtedly one of the factors that influences environments to a large extent. A good deal of information about ancient environments can be deduced from fossils, particularly

▼ Diagram showing the percentage of Foraminifera present in one rock sample

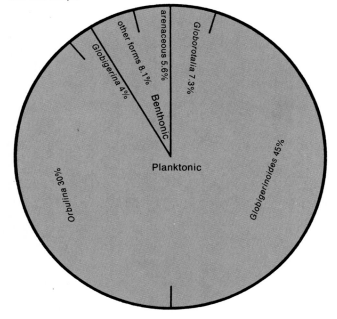

when they are of organisms that lived relatively recently and were the direct ancestors of forms now living, and which are known to favour specific climatic conditions. Some of the most obvious are perhaps fossil coral reefs, which are to be found in many parts of the world, including Britain, for example in the Cotswolds. Present-day coral reefs are restricted to the tropics, and there is no reason to suppose that coral reefs in the past were not also restricted to the tropics. Thus it is reasonable to suggest that the climate whenever the fossil coral reefs were growing was tropical.

A further example can be seen by the close study of fossil shells and foraminifera from the Mediterranean. The coastal waters of northern Europe are inhabited today by several species of shells and foraminifera that have also been found as fossils in the Mediterranean area in very recent rocks from the Pleistocene, about two million years old. Similarly, the coastal waters off Senegal and Nigeria contain shells that have also been found as fossils in Pleistocene rocks of a slightly different age in the same part of the Mediterranean. We know that several major

▼ An 'Arctic visitor': the bivalve *Arctica islandica* (see pp. 68, 238)

glaciations occurred at the beginning of the Pleistocene, which affected large areas of the northern hemisphere. They were separated by interglacial periods, and in some of these the climate of the Mediterranean area was very much warmer than it is now. During the glacial periods, the climate was considerably cooler. Depending upon whether the climate was warmer or cooler, the Mediterranean received 'visitors' from the warmer waters to the south, or from cooler ones to the north, and thus these fossils form very valuable indicators of oscillating climatic change. Pollen of Pleistocene plants can be used in a similar way, and this enables a sequence of vegetational zones for a particular area to be worked out and charts drawn from the information.

Biostratigraphy
It would be difficult to reconstruct the geological history of the Earth without the help of fossils, and biostratigraphy is concerned with the subdivision of rock sequences using fossils. Each geological period of the past 600 million years – the Phanerozoic Era – is characterized by typical suites of fossils. This enables us to date fossil-bearing rock strata of a particular area, and also to correlate these with those from other areas.

Fossils can be used to subdivide rock units very finely, and the smallest subdivision is called a zone. Zones can correspond to the range of an individual species, or to an assemblage of species – in this case known as an assemblage zone. In cases where a rock sequence contains a succession of species evolving one into another, the base of a zone is drawn at the first appearance of a new species. The base of the succeeding zone is where the subsequent species appears. Where there is not an evolutionary sequence present, a species might appear which has migrated into an area. Zoning on the basis of such fossils is often not as precise as using an evolutionary sequence, since the appearance of such species in different areas might not be quite contemporaneous.

By using several species to define a zone it is possible to cancel out, at least partly, some of the difficulties and possible errors that are linked with migration. There can be any number of zone permutations, since from time to time any rapidly-evolving fossil group may be used for zoning. Zonal boundaries established on the basis of different fossil groups often do not coincide.

A zone makes it possible to correlate rock sequences from different areas very accurately, but the problem is not as simple as it seems. Every organism in its different way shows signs of environmental influence, and this means that a species cannot have an unlimited distribution area. Therefore when rock sequences from different areas are compared there might have

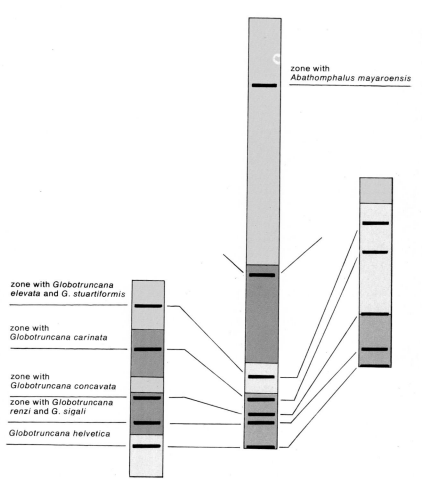

limestone with flints

limestone

marly limestone

marly limestone with flints

zone with *Abathomphalus mayaroensis*

zone with *Globotruncana elevata* and *G. stuartiformis*

zone with *Globotruncana carinata*

zone with *Globotruncana concavata*

zone with *Globotruncana renzi* and *G. sigali*

Globotruncana helvetica

▲ Example of zoning based on planktonic Foraminifera in sequences of Cretaceous rocks

69

been local environmental factors which make the flora and fauna different. The value of a fossil for zoning depends to what extent it is independent from its environment. Fossils of swimming or drifting organisms are much more useful for correlation purposes than are bottom-dwelling types. Rocks deposited in slightly different environments can be correlated by any fossil or fossil assemblage that is common to both.

Some of the best fossils for zoning and correlation, even from areas very far apart, include graptolites, ammonites, planktonic foraminifera and phytoplankton (planktonic plants). The chart on the previous page shows examples of zoning using planktonic foraminifera in Cretaceous rocks.

Palaeogeography
Finding out about the kind of environment extinct organisms inhabited is interesting, but what is undoubtedly more fascinating is to try to reassemble the jigsaw puzzle of their past distribution areas. This helps us to picture various parts of the Earth as it must

▲ *Mesosaurus brasiliensis*

have been in past ages, when things were very different.

Geography describes the present distribution of the Earth's land masses, seas, mountain ranges and the ocean basins. Palaeogeography does the same for the geological past and is a synthesis of the work of palaeoecologists, palaeoclimatologists, sedimentologists and biostratigraphers.

A great many detailed observations have to be made for a

▲ The gastropods *Strombus bubonius* and *Conus testudinarius*,
'tropical visitors' to the Mediterranean (see pp. 68, 238)

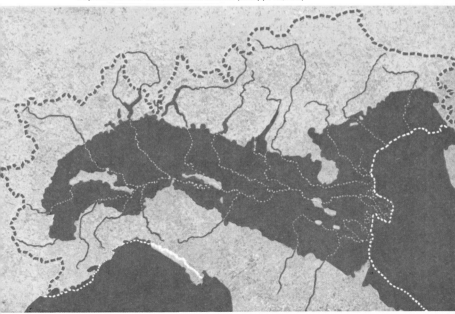

▲ The Gulf of Padua in the Pliocene

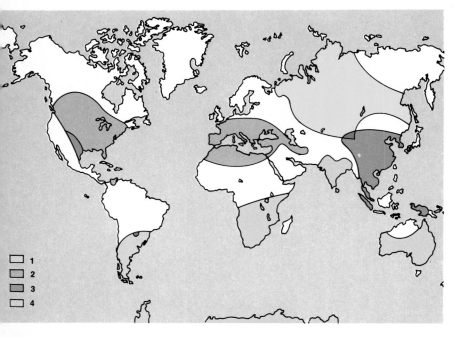

▲ Botanical zones in the late Carboniferous and Permian periods:
1. Angara; 2. Euroamerica; 3. Cathaysia; 4. Gondwana

palaeogeographical reconstruction to be really accurate, and accurate correlations between rock strata over a wide area are essential for meaningful results.

The following example from northern Italy will illustrate a palaeogeographical reconstruction. The plain of Padua is very recent, since it attained its current form only during the last two million years. Before that, in the Pliocene, there was a large gulf in its place, lapping the foot of the Alps in the north and west, and the northern edge of the Apennines in the south. This palaeogeographic picture of the area was produced by joining together all the points where contemporaneous sea-shore deposits containing fossils of marine molluscs were found. The resulting line demonstrated the rough position of the coastline of the ancient Gulf of Padua. The coastline that was drawn of the Paduan Gulf as a result of this research is reproduced on the previous page.

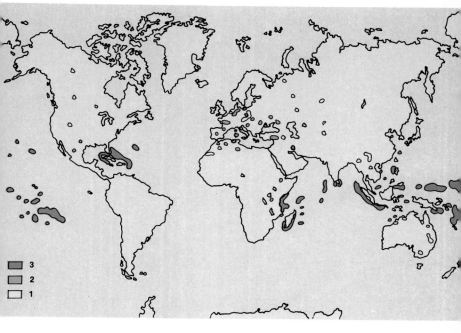

▲ Distribution of coral reefs in the Middle Devonian (1), the Jurassic (2), and at the present time (3)

Glossopteris leaves ▶

Pseudofossils

Sedimentary rocks commonly contain strange structures that at first sight look like fossils, but which are produced by inorganic processes, and are therefore not fossils at all. These interesting structures are known as pseudofossils.

Many examples of pseudofossils are known, and perhaps one of the most well-known is *Eozoon canadense*, found in ancient (Precambrian) rocks in Canada. For a long time *Eozoon* was regarded as one of the earliest forms of life. It is in fact composed of alternate layers of white calcite and green serpentine and resembles the stromatolite structures that are produced by some calcareous algae.

It was only when structures similar to *Eozoon canadense* were found in rocks of volcanic origin, that it was realized that *Eozoon* was not a fossil at all.

Another relatively common pseudofossil, *Paleodictyon*, illustrated on the next page, has a typical structure of hexagonal meshes. It is found in rocks from the Ordovician period to the Tertiary Era.

Dendrites are also common pseudofossils. These look like delicate branching plants, but the 'plants' have in fact been produced by manganese oxides and hydroxides percolating into the rocks containing them.

◀ *Paleodictyon*

▲ *Chondrites* and *Fucoides* (see page 150)
▼ *Eozoon canadense*

The Precambrian Era

The Precambrian Era is the first of the major subdivisions in the Earth's geological history. Its beginning corresponds with the origin of the Earth, about 4,600 million years ago. The oldest known rocks on Earth are about 3,800 million years old, and come from western Greenland. The Precambrian Era lasted some 4,000 million years, and represents nearly seven-eighths of the Earth's history.

Comparatively little is known about the Earth's history in these very remote times for several reasons. Because many of the Precambrian sedimentary rocks have been so altered by heat and pressure, their original structures have been lost. This makes it

difficult to find out the kind of environments such rocks were formed in, and any fossils they might have contained would be destroyed. Precambrian fossils are few and far between, and our picture of biological events in the Precambrian is scant.

The abundant fossil record is found in rocks younger than Precambrian. Life did exist before this time, but many of the organisms were microscopic. Most of the larger organisms were soft-bodied, and these only managed to produce fossils in rare circumstances.

Precambrian rocks basically occur in a few specific regions forming the cores of present continental masses, such as in the

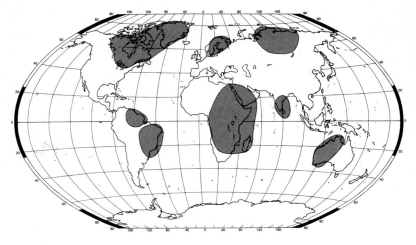

▲ Geographical distribution of Precambrian 'shields'

Baltic, Canada, Brazil, Africa and Australia. These areas are known as shields, and form stable regions where there have been no mountain-building episodes since the end of the era. The distribution of Precambrian shields is clearly shown on the map at the top of this page.

These shields carry traces of a great many ancient mountain ranges that have since been completely levelled by erosion through the ages. Precambrian rocks are not, however, restricted to these shields; they also lie beneath adjacent, more recent rock formations.

Many traces of climatic events have been found in rocks of the Precambrian Era. In Scandinavia, North America, South America and China, large deposits of Precambrian moraine material have been discovered, showing that glacial episodes or 'ice-ages' occurred long before the recent one.

There is enough good evidence to assume that during this first, very long geological era there was a very different atmosphere from the one we live in today. There was much less free oxygen in the atmosphere than there is today, and evidence of this has been found in the chemistry of various Precambrian rocks, in particular iron ores. A rise in the free oxygen content of the early atmosphere seems to have been caused, at least partly, by photosynthesis, the respiratory process which first developed in primitive plants (algae). These organisms, the most common at

▲ Specimens of *Vendia*

that time, may be said to have colonized the Earth and contributed towards preparing a favourable environment for all subsequent forms of life.

The first forms of life

Recent research carried out on rocks between 3,200 and 1,000 million years old from Africa, North America and Australia has enabled us to make intelligent suggestions as to the way life on Earth originated. But in spite of the fact that extremely important organisms have been found in these very old rocks the intriguing mystery cannot be regarded as solved, and perhaps it never will be possible to know all the answers.

There are many theories as to how life originated, probably at least 3,500 million years ago. Between the time the Earth's crust solidified and the appearance of the first organisms a process known as chemical evolution took place in the ancient oceans. This period is thought to have lasted several hundred million years, during which a special kind of chemical environment, a 'primordial soup' developed, which was rich in organic

▼ Stromatolites

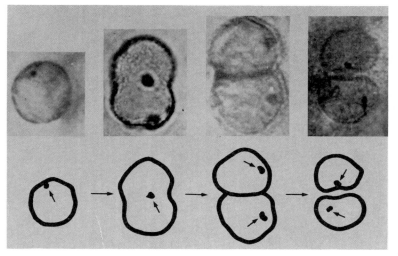

▲ Cell division in the green algae *Glenobotryodon*

▼ Laboratory-produced protocells similar to primitive Precambrian cells

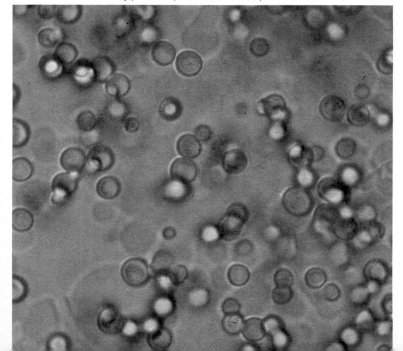

compounds – the precursors to the most primitive forms of life. As soon as these organic molecules accidentally joined together in a combination that led to the development of simple, primitive cells the first major step had been taken.

With the appearance of the first primitive cells, biological evolution began. The first organisms were probably very like

▲ *Corycium enigmaticum*

bacteria. They probably fed by absorbing nutritional substances from the surrounding water. The emergence of organisms capable of synthesizing organic substances led to oxygen being produced as a by-product of photosynthesis.

Some of the oldest known fossils come from Swaziland, from rocks estimated to be about 3,200 million years old. These are of microscopic one-celled organisms, and the cells lack a nucleus, and are called procaryotes. Evolution of organisms with cells with a nucleus (eucaryotes) took place very gradually. A study of fossils about 2,000 million years old from Ontario has revealed forms of organisms which appear to be very close to the transitional stage of cells without nuclei to those with nuclei.

The Ontario fossils, still represented by living bacteria and blue algae, have been classified into a large number of genera, among them *Gunflintia* and *Kakabekia*, and show that slight differentiation had already taken place in the biological world.

▲ Impression of the medusa *Brooksella alternata*

Some taxonomically uncertain organisms that have all been grouped under *Huroniosphaera* seem to indicate that evolution from procaryotic cells to eucaryotic cells (those with a nucleus) was imminent.

▼ The alga *Collenia*: left, internal structure; right, a fossil

Reliable evidence of cells with nuclei comes from sedimentary rocks some 1,000 million years old that have been discovered in northern Australia. The organisms found in these rocks have been classified as bacteria, blue algae, green algae and possibly fungi. Paelaeontologists have also been fortunate in being able to follow the various stages in the cellular subdivision of green algae belonging to the genus *Glenobotryodon*.

The illustration at the top of page 83 shows the main stages in the cell division of *Glenobotryodon*. The nucleus is the dark spot near the edge of the cell before and after division. Before the cell divides it moves to the centre, where it replicates and the two nuclei migrate to opposite poles; a new cell wall grows between the two.

With the appearance of eucaryotic one-celled organisms, evolution towards multicellular forms was rapid. Fossils have been found in more or less all areas containing Precambrian rocks. The evolutionary links between these primitive organisms and the later more advanced forms are difficult to establish in many cases, and there are usually considerable areas of doubt. One reason for this is the paucity of the fossil record in these very old rocks.

The plant world was to a large extent represented by algae, and these are the most widespread Precambrian fossils. Many of these fossils are actually stromatolites, strange layered structures secreted by the cells of certain of these primitive plants. A stromatolite is illustrated on page 82.

Examples of stromatolites include *Collenia*, *Cryptozoon*, *Greysonia* and *Newlandia*. A fossil specimen of *Collenia* is shown on page 85, together with an artist's impression of the internal structure of this algae.

A lot of Precambrian animal fossils are of soft-bodied forms, although *Vendia* has a hard skeleton, and resembles the later corals. The distinctive appearance of *Vendia* can be seen illustrated on page 81.

One of the richest sources of Precambrian fossils has been Ediacara in South Australia, where the rocks are about 600 million years old, not far below the base of the Cambrian. The fossils from this locality are soft-bodied forms, and are dominated by 'jellyfish' such as *Cyclomedusa* (the fossils are actually no more than impressions in sediment). There are also 'sea pens' such as *Rangea*, while *Spriggina* has a long segmented body and bears a vague resemblance to trilobites. Two of these fossil creatures, *Cyclomedusa plana* and *Spriggina*, are illustrated in the picture opposite.

The affinities of some of the fossils such as *Tribrachidium* (illustrated below) and *Parvacornia* are unknown.

Many Precambrian 'fossils' such as *Eozoon*, which has been mentioned earlier, have turned out to be pseudofossils. Other forms too have suffered this same fate including *Atikokania*, once thought to be a sponge, and *Camasia* and *Gallatinia* (which were originally described as algae).

Impressions of three late Precambrian fossils:
top left, *Cyclomedusa plana* (a 'jellyfish');
bottom left, *Tribrachidium*;
bottom right, *Spriggina* (an annelid)

The Palaeozoic Era

The Palaeozoic Era is the second major chapter in the Earth's geological history and the first phase of the Phanerozoic. The name of the era comes from the Greek *palaios* (old) and *zoon* (living), referring to the fact that these rocks contain the earliest abundant fossil record.

This era lasted about 350 million years and is subdivided into six periods: Cambrian, Ordovician, Silurian, Devonian, Carboniferous and Permian. In North America the Carboniferous is divided into two systems, the Mississippian and Pennsylvanian.

Two major mountain-building episodes occurred during the Palaeozoic Era and in the process a great many mountain ranges

were formed all over the world. The first cycle, which is known as the Caledonian, took place between the Cambrian period and the end of the Silurian. Mountains which have their origins in this cycle include those in Scandinavia, the North American Appalachians, the highlands of Scotland, the Lake District and Snowdonia. At the end of the Caledonian cycle land and sea distribution was very different from the arrangement at its beginning. The Baltic and Canadian shields became joined together by a range of high mountains running from what is present-day Scandinavia, through Scotland, Ireland, North Wales, and also south-westward into the Appalachians.

▲ A Devonian trilobite and starfish preserved in pyrite

The second mountain-building cycle, known as the Variscan, lasted from Devonian to Permian times. Typical Variscan ranges include the Ardennes, the Vosges, the Black Forest, the Bohemian Massif and the Urals. When the Urals were formed at the end of the Permian period, the North Atlantic Continent fused with the continent of Angara, which was more or less the same as present northern Asia. In the southern hemisphere lay a vast ancient continent known as Gondwanaland, comprising land masses that now make up most of South America, Africa, Madagascar, India, Australia and Antarctica.

Between the Carboniferous and Permian periods there was a major ice-age. Ancient deposits of moraine material (tillites) dating from this period have been found on land masses that once formed part of Gondwanaland. The present distribution of these tillites at one time caused heated debate about the size and location of the ice caps. Looking at the present distribution of land in the southern hemisphere, it is impossible to envisage that a single enormous ice cap as large or nearly as large as a hemisphere could have formed. Two very important geological

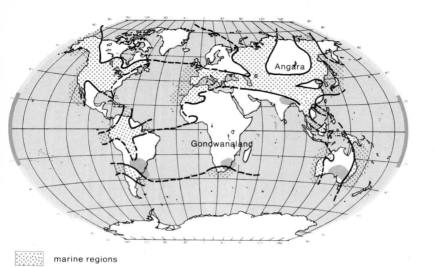

marine regions

areas showing traces of glaciation

▲ Land and sea distribution during the Permo-Carboniferous glaciation

events in Earth's history – continental drift and polar migration –
have enabled us to explain this apparent mystery.

If Africa, South America, India, Australia and Antarctica were
all pushed together, this ice cap would become much smaller.
Palaeomagnetic measurements show that during Permo-
Carboniferous times the position of the poles was different, one
lay near the southern tip of Africa and the other in the middle of
the Pacific Ocean. The position of the South Pole fits in well with
the geographic centre of the southern ice cap, whereas the
position of the North Pole would explain why no traces of a
northern ice cap have been found. During the Carboniferous
period huge coal deposits were formed in North America, in a belt
across central Europe, in the Ukraine and in China – regions that
were then close to the Equator or lay not very far from it.

Several crucial events in evolutionary history occurred during
the Palaeozoic Era. The first was the apparent 'explosion' of life
that took place at the beginning of the Cambrian period, when
trilobites and many other invertebrate animals appeared. The
second event occurred in the later part of the Silurian period when

life first appeared on land. Vertebrates probably appeared during the Ordovician period. At first they were completely aquatic, but from the beginning of the late Devonian period there were also terrestrial forms.

By the end of the Permian period all the groups of invertebrate animals had appeared. Birds and mammals were the only vertebrates still to come, while angiosperms were the only important group of plants that had still not appeared.

The biological explosion

The sudden appearance of a large number of groups of animals and plants at the beginning of the Palaeozoic Era is one of the most extraordinary aspects of evolutionary history. The sea had been the cradle of life until the end of the Precambrian Era. It was at that time inhabited by rather strange organisms whose evolutionary links with Palaeozoic organisms have been difficult to establish except in a few cases. So far, it is only possible to give hypothetical answers as to why this should be so.

The relative scarcity of Precambrian fossils compared with the much larger numbers to be found in rocks of the Cambrian period can be explained in several ways. One reason might be that the end of the Precambrian Era was characterized by intense mountain-building activity, accompanied by major retreats of the sea, perhaps partly connected with a great deterioration of the climate and associated ice-age. There must have been very few favourable conditions for the survival of animal and plant remains at this time.

It must also be remembered that the Precambrian rocks were to a large extent considerably altered by heat and pressure, which means that potential fossils would have been destroyed. Possibly, very few potentially fossil-bearing rocks from just before the Cambrian period managed to survive.

These suggestions offer only a partial solution. On the level of evolution there also seems to be a sudden 'jump' between the few primitive organisms that existed at the end of the Precambrian Era and the very large number of genera and species that characterized the beginning of the Palaeozoic Era. It seems as if many different groups of organisms acquired hard, potentially fossilizable, parts early in the Cambrian period composed principally of either silica, calcium carbonate, chitin or phosphates. It seems as if most Precambrian organisms were unable to form hard skeletal parts, and thus only a minute proportion survived as fossils.

One of the most surprising events that characterized the beginning of the Palaeozoic Era was the appearance of large

The Devonian trilobite *Phacops rana* ▶

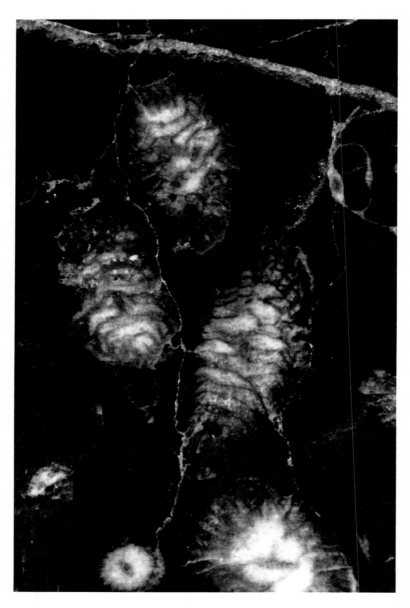

▲ Thin section of a tetracoral

▲ The articulate brachiopod *Spirifer*

numbers of trilobite species. These advanced arthropods had an exoskeleton composed chiefly of calcium carbonate and were very important during the early part of the era. The roots of this group of arthropods is unknown. Another group of arthropods, which bear a certain resemblance to the trilobites is known as the trilobitoids. These are now thought to belong to several independent groups. Their existence is known from finds made in

▼ The graptolite *Spirograptus*

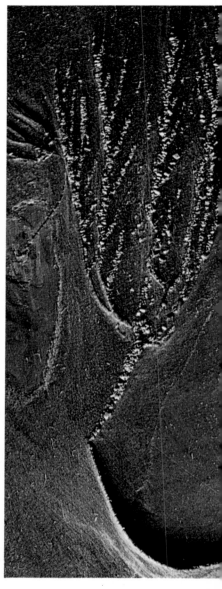

▲ The Carboniferous plant *Rhacopteris*　　　▲ The crinoid *Rhadinocrinus dactylus*

the Cambrian Burgess shale of British Columbia. Most trilobitoids had no hard parts. They only managed to fossilize because they were buried rapidly in fine-grained sediment.

The discovery of trilobitoids is really very interesting. They emphasize the vast number of organisms not normally fossilized which existed alongside those which do, and they demonstrate the rapid evolution and diversification taking place early in the Cambrian.

▼ A Permian cotylosaur, *Labidosaurus harmatus*

Life in the sea

While we know comparatively little about the animals and plants of the Precambrian Era, our knowledge of those of the Palaeozoic Era is much greater, even though the picture is much more complicated.

Some of the first forms of life developing in the sea in the Precambrian Era were plants. During the Palaeozoic Era marine plants did not increase to any great extent. They are represented by Cyanophyceae (blue algae), Phaenophyceae (brown algae), Chlorophyceae (green algae) and Rhodophyceae (red algae). Almost all these marine groups had evolutionary links with primitive Precambrian forms, and they are still in existence. Green algae, represented by the Codiaceae and Dasycladaceae, and red algae, represented by the Solenoporaceae, became particularly important from the beginning of the Silurian period onwards. Because they were able to 'fix' calcium carbonate into a

▼ The Ordovician trilobite *Lloydolithus ornatus*

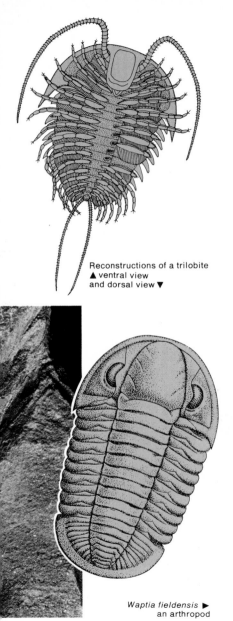

Reconstructions of a trilobite
▲ ventral view
and dorsal view ▼

Waptia fieldensis ►
an arthropod

99

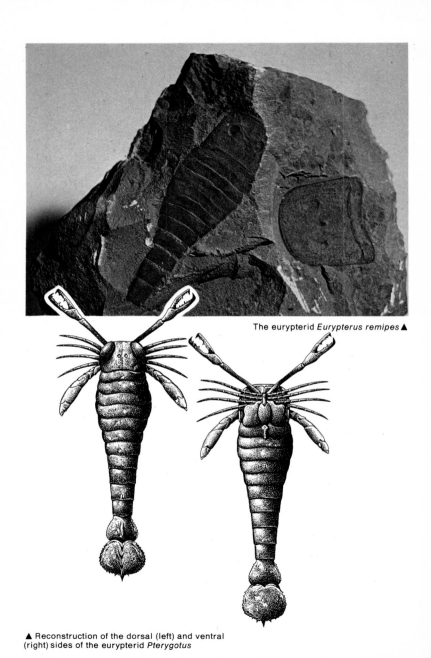

The eurypterid *Eurypterus remipes* ▲

▲ Reconstruction of the dorsal (left) and ventral
(right) sides of the eurypterid *Pterygotus*

▲ The Devonian brachiopod *Spinocyrtia* (dorsal views)

kind of external skeleton, many of these algae became important
as rock-formers during the Palaeozoic Era and later.

As far as animals are concerned, almost all the marine
invertebrate groups were in existence in the Cambrian period, or
appeared during the course of the early part of the Palaeozoic
Era. The Protozoa were represented in the Cambrian period
mainly by the Radiolaria (micro-organisms with a siliceous shell),
some of which have remained almost unchanged down to the
present day. The Foraminifera are important as zone fossils in
some Palaeozoic rocks, particularly the fusulinids. These large
foraminifera had an elongated, spindle-shaped shell made of
calcite and inhabited warm, shallow seas in Carboniferous and
Permian times.

The sponges are some of the most primitive multicellular
invertebrates. A sponge is typically composed of a collection of
differentiated cells, which puts them halfway between the
Protozoa and Metazoa. The parts of a sponge that generally
fossilize are the spicules, small siliceous or calcareous elements
that formed a reticulate framework acting as an internal skeleton.
Several sponge genera inhabited the sea from the beginning of the
Cambrian period, possibly even before.

Archaeocyathids were also common in the Cambrian seas.
They are problematic organisms and were at one time thought to
be sponges, but are now regarded as a distinct group of animals
that became extinct. They have a conical body composed of two
concentric calcareous cones held together with vertical and
horizontal plates, and attached themselves to the sea bed by
means of anchorage spines.

Another important group are the coelenterates. These organisms have two clearly distinct forms: free-living or medusoid (jellyfish) and anchored or polyp forms (sea-anemone-like). Although many did not readily fossilize, being soft-bodied, the oldest coelenterate fossil specimens belong to free-living forms and have been classified as the class Protomedusae. They were well represented by the genus *Brooksella*, whose impressions have been found in the Precambrian and fairly commonly in rocks of the Cambrian, Ordovician, and Silurian periods.

Polyp coelenterate forms with strong colonial habits include the Hydrozoa, the order Stromatoporoidea being particularly important from the beginning of the Cambrian period onwards.

During the Ordovician the corals became important. These coelenterates secreted a hard skeleton, and were represented by solitary as well as by colonial forms, the latter being particularly important as reef builders. The corals are subdivided into various

▼ The Silurian tabulate coral *Halysites catenularis*

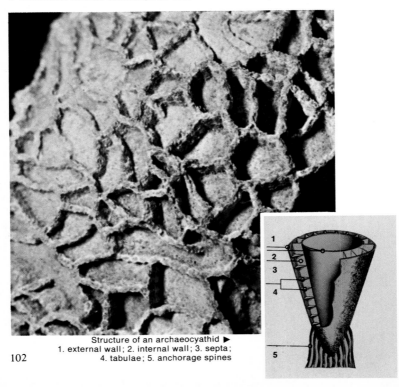

Structure of an archaeocyathid ▶
1. external wall; 2. internal wall; 3. septa;
4. tabulae; 5. anchorage spines

orders that also include living corals. Tetracorals (or rugosans) were exclusively Palaeozoic, and at the time they were important. However, by the end of the era they had become extinct.

Tabulate corals are difficult to relate to others. They were very characteristic colonial organisms that appeared in the Ordovician period, and *Halysites* is a typical example. The Ordovician also saw the rise of the bryozoans, a group of rather problematic organisms, particularly as far as their taxonomic position is concerned. They comprise a series of small polyps with a calcareous skeleton and lived together in colonies which superficially resemble certain corals.

Brachiopods are in some aspects of their internal structure like bryozoans. The first rather primitive forms of these marine invertebrates had appeared in the Cambrian period, or possibly even before, and throughout the rest of the Palaeozoic Era they inhabited the continental shelves in abundance. Brachiopods have

▼ A Devonian tetracoral colony

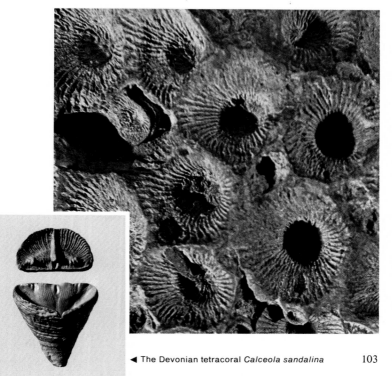

◀ The Devonian tetracoral *Calceola sandalina*   103

a characteristic bivalved shell typically composed of an inflated ventral valve with a perforated umbo and a rather smaller dorsal valve. A fleshy peduncle passes through the umbo aperture and the organism uses this to attach itself to the ocean floor. In the inarticulate classes the two valves are held together by muscles alone whereas in the articulate classes there is a complex hinge mechanism. Examples of the Devonian brachiopod *Spinocyrtia* are illustrated on page 101.

▼ The Ordovician bryozoan *Pseudohornea bifida*

▲ Exterior view and cross-section of the
Silurian sponge *Astylospongia praemorsa*

▲ The Middle Cambrian annelid *Canadia setigera*

Inarticulates are undoubtedly the most primitive brachiopods and during the Ordovician period and subsequently, they were represented, among others, by the genus *Lingula*.

Articulate brachiopods are far more important and are subdivided into six major groups or orders, all of which appeared during the Palaeozoic Era. The order Pentamerida (typified by the genus *Pentamerus*) appeared in the Cambrian period and became extinct towards the end of the Devonian; the Orthida which also appeared in the Cambrian survived until the end of the Permian period (they include the characteristic genus *Orthis*, which was widespread, particularly during the Ordovician period). The Spiriferida, Strophomenida and Rhynchonellida survived to the end of the era. The most typical genera in the order Spiriferida were *Spirifer*, which is rather common in Devonian and Carboniferous rocks and had a characteristic shell with a long, straight hinge-line, and the Devonian genus *Uncites*, which has a very prominent curved umbo.

The order Strophomenida includes a rather large group of families, some of which were particularly important, such as the richtofenids. This family includes several Permian genera that had radically modified their shell to become coral-like. The genus *Productus*, which existed from the Upper Devonian to the Carboniferous periods, and the genus *Strophomena* also belong to this order. The order Rhynchonellida was represented by forms with a shell carrying rather pronounced radial ridges (plications).

The last brachiopod order, the Terebratulida, appeared in the Devonian period and like the Rhynchonellida it includes species that are still in existence.

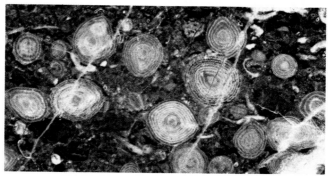

▲ A thin section of Permian rock with fusulinids
(*Neoschwagerina craticulifera*)

Brachiopods occupied a very important place among
Palaeozoic invertebrates, and the number of species and
individuals inhabiting the continental shelves was enormous.
During the Mesozoic Era bivalves tended to supplant the
brachiopods in many of their habitats.

Another important group of organisms that occurred in the
Palaeozoic Era can all be included under the term 'worms',
although this term does not have any taxonomic significance. The
term actually embraces several distinct groups (though they do
have similar characteristics), as well as problematic organisms
that may possibly be connected with them but are difficult to
identify. Conodonts are sometimes included. They are jaw-like or
tooth-like microfossils made of phosphate. Many scientists regard
them as tiny worm jaws, but the parent animal remains unknown.

Fossils of complete worm bodies have been found in rocks
from as early as the Cambrian period. They include the marine
worms (Chaetognatha), which have a cylindrical body and paired
antennae. The Middle Cambrian Burgess shales have yielded only
one chaetognath genus, *Amiskwia*. The Sipunculoidea, which
appeared at the same time as chaetognaths, are also very
interesting. The Burgess shale contains other extremely
interesting annelids, among them the polychaetes, which include
three fairly common fossil orders. There are the vagrants (soft-
bodied marine worms), represented by small jaw-like fossils
known as scolecodonts, found from Ordovician times onwards.
Sessile worms are a much more important and better known
order, including many 'burrow' fossils, and forms which secreted
calcareous tubes such as the Devonian genus *Hicetes*, which lived

in symbiosis with the coral *Pleurodictyum*. The third order, the Miscoidea, was represented by very interesting species, which were found mainly at Burgess. The order, which became extinct in the Ordovician period, was mainly represented by *Canadia*, *Miskoia* and *Wiwaxia*.

The onychoporans were represented during the Cambrian period by the genus *Aysheaia*, which is similar to living members of the group, although the latter have adapted to living in a terrestrial environment.

Arthropods are especially important Palaeozoic invertebrates. They are subdivided into a great many classes that also include terrestrial forms. The trilobitoids appeared during the Cambrian period, but became extinct during the Devonian. As mentioned earlier, several independent groups are included under this heading. They include the merostome-like *Sidneyia*, crustacean-like *Burgessia* and *Waptia*, and trilobite-like *Naraoia* and *Marrella*; all are from the Burgess shale. It is possible that these groups may include the roots of several later arthropod groups.

Trilobites are some of the most common of fossil arthropods. They were already well developed on their appearance in the early Cambrian fossil record, and became extinct at the end of the Permian, without leaving any descendants. Trilobites typically have a flat, slightly oval calcareous exoskeleton that is longitudinally divided into three lobes, one median and two lateral. The exoskeleton can also be divided into the head (or cephalon), the thorax, and the tail (or pygidium). Each of these parts is composed of a number of segments which in the case of the cephalon and pygidium are fused together. The central inflated portion of the cephalon is called the glabella, on either side of which the eyes are situated. Trilobites had a series of rather simple appendages attached to their underside, each comprising a walking leg and gill branch. Some of those on the cephalon became modified as simple mouthparts and as antennae. Many trilobites were able to roll themselves up into a ball, like modern woodlice and pill bugs.

There is an enormous variety of trilobites known, the Cambrian genera such as *Agnostus*, *Olenus* and *Paradoxides* being useful zone fossils. Trilobites managed to adapt to many different modes of life but it is thought that most lived on, or close to, the sea bed. We can deduce that others, with enormous eyes, were undoubtedly swimmers.

The merostomes, which appeared during the Cambrian period, are another very important arthropod class, and include the eurypterids or sea-scorpions. Some of the earlier forms were marine, but later ones gradually adapted to brackish and fresh

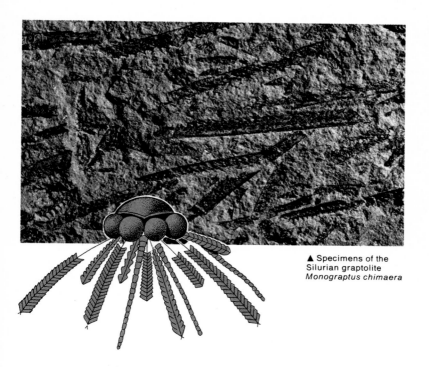

▲ Specimens of the
Silurian graptolite
Monograptus chimaera

▲ Reconstruction of a hypothetical graptolite colony (see p. 114)

water. They were represented by genera such as *Eurypterus* and
Pterygotus, and became extinct during the Permian period.
Crustaceans appeared as early as the Cambrian period, but they
seem to have remained in comparatively small numbers
throughout the Palaeozoic Era.

Molluscs appeared in the Cambrian, and by the Ordovician all
the classes into which they are subdivided were represented.
Monoplacophoran molluscs, such as in the genus *Pilina*,
appeared during the Cambrian and have a simple conical shell.
They were thought to have become extinct by the end of the
Devonian period until the exciting discovery of living specimens
in the Pacific Ocean in the 1950s.

The amphineura appeared in the Ordovician, as did the
scaphopods or tusk-shells. Bivalves (also known as
lamellibranchs) are known from Cambrian rocks, and all the

▲ The Devonian starfish *Euzonosoma*

groups now in existence had become established by the end of the
Silurian. All the living orders of gastropods (snails) were also
represented during the Palaeozoic Era. Like the bivalves,
however, they were not as abundant as they were to become after
the end of the Palaeozoic.

Nautiloids, the only members of the cephalopod class (which
includes modern octopus and squid) that were widespread by the
later part of the Cambrian period, became fairly important.
Nautiloids, with their straight, slightly curved or coiled shell, were
typically pelagic organisms and became very widespread during
the Palaeozoic Era, particularly members of the straight-shelled
group called orthocones.

Ammonoids, derived from the nautiloids, appeared during the
late Devonian, the most important being the goniatites and the
clymenids. The first became particularly widespread in the
Carboniferous period, while the second was exclusively
Devonian. Like the nautiloids, the ammonoids were pelagic, and
are particularly useful as zone fossils.

▲ The Devonian starfish *Furcaster palaeozoicus*

The Silurian edrioasteroid *Edrioaster* ▲

▲ The Silurian bivalve *Cardioloa cornucopiae*

▼ Calyx of the Carboniferous blastoid *Pentremites*

▼ Devonian nautiloid *Cyrtoceras lineatum*

▲ The Carboniferous bivalve *Posidonomya*

113

Echinoderms (the group including modern starfish and sea-urchins) were also very common marine creatures in Palaeozoic times. They are divided into a number of classes, many of which became extinct during or at the end of the era, and included both free-swimming and sedentary forms. The many minor groups present in the Palaeozoic include the sea-urchin-like edrioasteroids, the stalked cystoids and blastoids. The edrioasteroids appeared in the Cambrian and became extinct in the Carboniferous (they included sessile forms with no peduncle such as *Edrioaster*). The cystoids, which appeared in the Ordovician period and disappeared in the Devonian, included forms that were attached to the sea bed by means of a peduncle supporting a pseudospherical theca. The blastoids were similar, appearing at the same time, but did not become extinct until the Permian period (*Pentremites* was the most widespread and typical genus). The crinoids, or sea-lilies are much more common and widespread, and vaguely resemble a slender-armed starfish anchored to the sea bed by a long stalk. Fragments of this stalk are extremely common fossils, sometimes almost entirely making up some limestone beds – known as crinoidal limestone. Representatives of the group still survive today.

Free-living echinoderms include the Stelleroidea or starfish, which were represented by a great many genera by the end of the Ordovician period, among them *Euzonosoma* and *Furcaster*. We also have fossil evidence of Holothuroidea or sea cucumbers from as early as the Cambrian period, mainly in the form of small skeletal elements which supported the soft, fleshy body. The Echinoidea, or sea-urchins, appeared in the Ordovician period, but remained in small numbers only throughout the rest of the Palaeozoic.

The graptolites are a group of exclusively Palaeozoic organisms whose relationships were a complete mystery until the discovery of exceptionally well-preserved specimens. They are now believed to be related to the hemichordates. They were particularly important during the Ordovician and Silurian periods and left fossils that look like faint pencil marks. Graptolites were colonial animals, and included forms that attached themselves to the sea bed, and other which floated freely in the oceans. Some forms of graptolite were believed to have been attached to a special 'float', although this interpretation has been disputed by some authorities.

The illustration on page 109 shows specimens of the Silurian graptolite *Monograptus chimaera*, together with a reconstruction of a hypothetical colony. A spiral type of graptolite, *Spirograptus*, is pictured on page 95.

▲ Silurian marine diorama

▼ Devonian marine diorama

▲ The Devonian placoderm *Dinichthys*

The Devonian chondrichthyian *Cladoselache* ▶

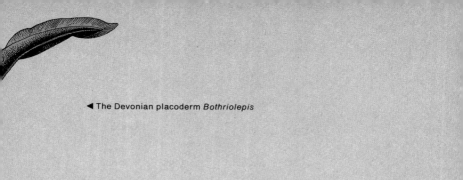

◄ The Devonian placoderm *Bothriolepis*

▼ The Devonian placoderm *Pterichthyodes*

Early vertebrates

The earliest known fossil vertebrates date back to the Ordovician. They are remains of primitive jawless fishes belonging to a group called agnathans, which includes present-day lampreys and hagfish. The Palaeozoic agnathans are commonly known as ostracoderms, and had a skeleton of cartilage and their skin was covered with a large number of thick scales (those covering the head commonly became fused to form a protective headshield). The mouth was situated on the underside of the head. Ostracoderms are unlikely to have been fast swimmers, and moved by wiggling the flexible tail from side to side. They probably lived close to the bottom, feeding on organic debris. Although still quite primitive, the ostracoderms posessed a well-organized central nervous system.

There is a gap in the fossil fish record from the Ordovician to the late Silurian. By this time, there were three main groups of ostracoderms, the cephalaspids, pteraspids and anaspids. The cephalaspids, which were numerically the most important, had a dorso-ventrally flattened headshield and one pair of fins. The rest of the body was covered in scales and ended in a straight tail with a larger upper lobe.

Pteraspids were broadly torpedo-shaped fish, and the nostrils were positioned on the underside of the head, there were no paired fins and the tail had a larger lower lobe.

The anaspid group had a laterally compressed body which was covered with symmetrical scales, and a tail with a larger lower lobe; these fish might have been the only nektonic (living away from the sea bed) ostracoderms.

By the late Silurian and early Devonian, the agnathans were accompanied by three other groups of fish. The placoderms were some of the most primitive jawed fishes, and they appeared during the late Silurian. The jaw was evolved by modification of one of the gill arches, and a series of paired fins developed from skin folds with cartilaginous supports. Like some ostracoderms, they had a thick bony covering of the head. Some placoderms reached a vast size, and some examples of *Dinichthys* were over 10 metres long, and were probably ferocious predators. An artist's impression of the *Dinichthys*, and other placoderms, can be seen on pages 116–17.

The chondrichthyans had a skeleton made of cartilage, and include present-day sharks and rays. They included freshwater and marine forms. The primitive sharks, such as *Hybodus* were exclusively marine, and the teeth are common as fossils.

The third group, the osteichthyans or bony fish, includes a vast majority of present-day fish. There are two groups within the

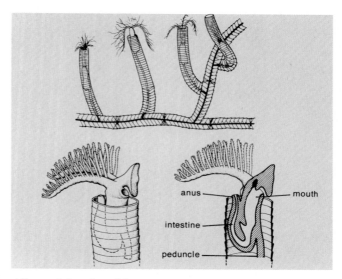

▲ Top: part of a colony of the hemichordate *Rhabdopleura*.
Below left: detail of a single specimen; below right; specimen in section

anus — mouth

intestine

peduncle

osteichthyans – one includes the familiar ray-finned fish; the other
the lung fish or dipnoans and the lobe-fins or crossopterygians.
The latter are particularly important, because they include the
ancestors of the amphibians.

The origin of the vertebrates is one of the mysteries that
remains to be solved. The early fish described above were already
highly organized, and this certainly suggests that their ancestors
should be sought in still earlier deposits.

The first life on land
Life remained tied to an aquatic environment for a very long time.
Invertebrates, vertebrates and plants all had their origins there,
but between the end of the Silurian and the end of the Devonian
periods all three groups had representatives which had begun to
move on to dry land. From fossil evidence, the first organisms that
lived in a terrestrial environment were bacteria, fungi, mosses,
myriapods (millipedes) and scorpions belonging to the genus
Palaeophonus. This event in evolutionary history occurred during
the late Silurian period. We know very little about how these

organisms evolved from living in water to living on dry land. The plants previously mentioned might have originated from primitive one-celled forms then in existence, since the most highly evolved algae of the period, the Dasycladaceans, possibly evolved into the higher plants. Scorpions probably have their origins in the eurypterids, which were widespread at this time.

Perhaps the most spectacular event in the conquest of land was the appearance of the amphibians. The development of jaws and paired fins were important stages in vertebrate history. The development of efficient fins meant that fishes were no longer restricted to areas close to the ocean floor but could move permanently into the open sea. The next step was to breathe oxygen and move on to dry land.

Amphibians appear to have evolved directly from freshwater crossopterygian fishes and appeared during the Devonian period. Their evolution must be set in the geographical and environmental context of the northern hemisphere at that time. Not long before, in late Silurian times, a large land mass known as the North Atlantic Continent had formed. Large tracts of it were covered by desert. There were many coastal lakes and lagoons in which freshwater crossopterygian fishes flourished. In long periods of drought these basins would dry up. Unless the fish could somehow manage to adapt themselves to this new environment, the consequences would obviously be fatal. Living species of African, Australian and American lung-fish or dipnoans live in similar environments, which periodically dry up. In periods of drought they burrow into the soft mud at the bottom and coat themselves in mucus to retain moisture and wait for the water to return, when they again return to their former environment.

For the Devonian crossopterygian fishes the solution was to adapt to living out of the water, at least temporarily, but there

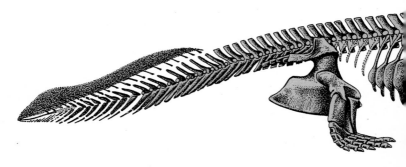

▲ Reconstruction of the early Permian amphibian *Diplocaulus*

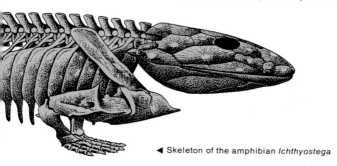

◀ Skeleton of the amphibian *Ichthyostega*

▲ Reconstruction of *Rhynia major*
(see p. 131)

▲ Reconstruction of *Asteroxylon*
(see p. 131)

were several major obstacles. They had to evolve a method of
breathing air, using their swim-bladder as a lung, but this was not
enough. They had to be able to move, since they needed to reach
water, which was essential for parts of the life-cycle, including
reproduction, and also to prevent prolonged exposure to the air
dehydrating their skin. The paired fins acted as the first
rudimentary limbs.

Paradoxically their need to stay close to water led primitive
tetrapods on to dry land. The early amphibians found themselves
in a virgin environment that gave them enormous scope to
expand, since there were no other competitors apart from other
amphibians. Throughout much of the remainder of the
Palaeozoic Era they stayed the almost unchallenged masters of
dry land, at least along the edge of the sea, and near the rivers
and lakes.

Primitive amphibians are collectively known as
Labyrinthodonts because of their typical labyrinthine tooth
structure. They are divided into several major groups. The
ichthyostegids were directly descended from crossopterygian

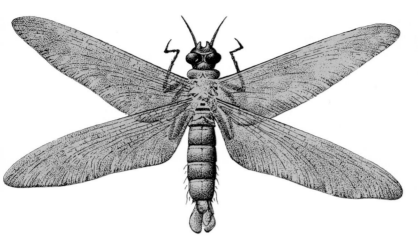

▲ Reconstruction of *Meganeura*, an insect from the Carboniferous forests

fishes and all other amphibians eventually evolved from them. The genus *Ichthyostega* was little more than one metre long, and still had a fairly high skull, a long caudal fin supported by bony ribs and five-toed limbs. Its way of life was still very much tied to the water. During the Carboniferous period several groups of amphibians emerged. The embolomeres are probably close to the group from which reptiles evolved, and survived to the early Permian period.

The amphibians best adapted to life out of the water were a group of thick-set animals, which had a rather flattened skull with a double occipital condyle, like all living members of the class. Typical of the group were *Eryops*, which could be as long as two metres, and *Cacops*, which was less than half a metre long.

The Stereospondyli were the last labyrinthodont amphibians to appear. They evolved from the *Eryops* group in the late Permian period, becoming extinct towards the end of the succeeding Triassic. They re-adapted to living in the water and so to a certain extent they had regressed in relation to their immediate ancestors. The Stereospondyli include the largest amphibians in the world. It

▲ The Devonian crossopterygian fish *Eusthenopteron*

is now generally believed that the Anura, the group that includes frogs and toads, evolved from the labyrinthodonts. However the first true anurans do not seem to have appeared until the beginning of the Mesozoic Era.

All labyrinthodonts had vertebrae that went through a cartilaginous stage before becoming changed into bone. Members of another amphibian group, the Lepospondyli, had vertebrae which were made from bone in all stages of development. The Lepospondyli were in existence mainly in Carboniferous and Permian times. They were never very common, remained small and were barely adapted to living on dry land. Some curious forms evolved from them, for example the early Permian *Diplocaulus*. This creature had a salamander-like body and an enormous, triangular skull (this was caused by the bones at the back of the skull extending out towards the sides). *Dolichosoma* was another strange genus. It lived in late Carboniferous times and had a completely limbless body like a snake.

▼ Skeleton of the Permian amphibian *Eryops megacephalus*

Reconstruction of the Carboniferous amphibian *Diplovertebron* ▶

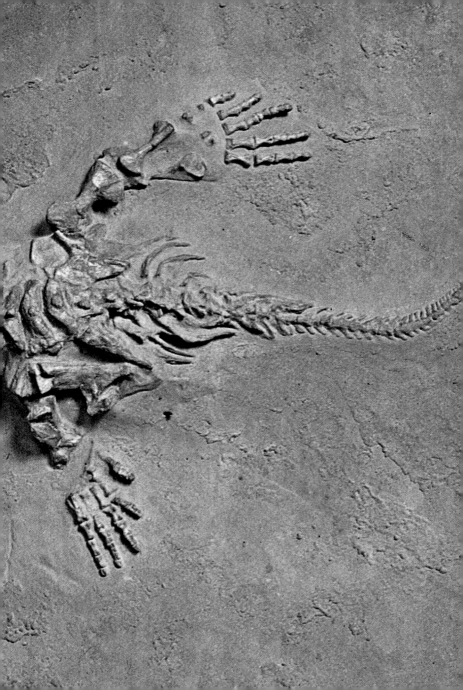

The emergence of reptiles

When amphibians evolved on to dry land they were able to spread, branch out and evolve to an unlimited degree as they had no other competitors apart from other amphibians. So during the course of the Carboniferous and Permian periods, amphibians divided into several groups, strengthening their new-won position and colonizing vast areas of the world. But this very strong evolutionary capability was, in a way, their greatest enemy. One group gave rise to the better adapted reptiles, which were eventually to replace the amphibians as the dominant vertebrates on land. To all intents and purposes the period of amphibian dominance was practically over by the end of the Palaeozoic Era,

▲ *Tridentinosaurus antiquus*, a Permian protorosaur reptile

since reptiles left very little room for other land vertebrates in the next era, which is sometimes called the 'Age of Reptiles'.

One of the ways in which reptiles differ from amphibians is in the type of egg they produce, although this cannot be shown by palaeontological evidence. Amphibians had to stay more or less tied to the water for all their basic functions, particularly reproduction. Reptiles successfully abandoned the water and it was essentially the amniote egg that made this possible. The egg could be laid on dry land instead of water because the embryo contained reserves of nutritional substances and was able to absorb oxygen from the outside through a porous shell.

Although fossilized reptile eggs have been found, they are very

◀ Preceding pages: *Seymouria baylorensis*, a Permian amphibian rare. To tell a reptile from an amphibian there is no choice but to go by the skeletal characteristics. Fortunately reptiles and amphibians are very different in bone structure. The reptile skull tends to be compressed laterally rather than flattened and contains fewer bones than an amphibian skull. It also has typical temporal openings, which serve the dual purpose of reducing the skull's weight and leaving room for the muscles to operate the lower jaw. The different position of these temporal openings is used as a basis in reptile classification. The skull is joined on to the spinal column by means of a single condyle. The rest of the reptile skeleton basically follows the amphibian pattern, although there are differences in the structure of the limbs.

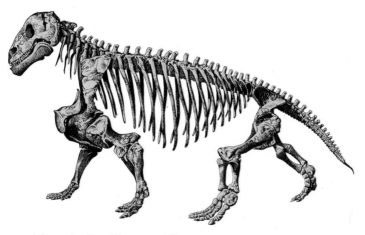

▲ Reconstruction of the mammal-like reptile *Moschops capensis*

No information is available about the various transitional stages between amphibians and reptiles, but there can no longer be any doubt that reptiles evolved from amphibians. However, one group of Carboniferous and Permian animals, typified by *Seymouria*, shared many amphibian and reptilian characteristics. They have therefore sometimes been classified as amphibians and sometimes as reptiles. Nevertheless they are not a 'missing link' connecting the two classes, but a sterile evolutionary side branch. *Seymouria* has an amphibian skull while the rest of its skeleton is more characteristically reptilian (similar limb structure and sacral vertebrae joined together and incorporated into the sacral bone). Apart from ichthyosaurs, all the important reptile groups had appeared by the end of the Palaeozoic. These were the Anapsida, Lepidosauria, Archosauria, Euryapsida and Synapsida.

The Anapsida contains the most primitive reptiles, the cotylosaurs, which were in existence from the middle of the Carboniferous to Triassic times, and all other reptile groups evolved from them. Cotylosaurs are divided into two groups: captorhinomorphs, which were exclusively Palaeozoic, and diadectimorphs, which survived into the Triassic. The first group includes the Permian genus *Limoscelis*, which still had labyrinthine teeth and is thought to have been a carnivorous predator about one and a half metres long. The diadectimorphs were all herbivorous, but had a heavier and bulkier frame than captorhinomorphs and were larger. The Permian *Pareiasaurus* from South Africa and Russia was nearly three metres long; while *Diadectus*, from the North American Permian rocks, was slightly shorter.

The idea that the other anapsid group, the Chelonia (which includes turtles and tortoises), may have evolved from cotylosaurs is somewhat controversial, because the first true chelonians that appeared in the Triassic period were already well specialized. An animal that could have been a chelonian ancestor, *Eunotosaurus*, was found in Permian rocks in South Africa. It had teeth and a long, flexible neck, but (and this is perhaps its most interesting aspect) its dorsal ribs were so wide they touched each other along the edges. This structure could have been a primitive forerunner of what was eventually to become in later ages a turtle carapace.

Lepidosaurians, to which many living reptile species belong, were represented in Palaeozoic times by small lizard-like creatures. They were very primitive, but had a diapsid skull (a skull with two temporal openings). They belonged to the order Eosuchia, the most typical genus being *Youngina*. Archosaurs became lords of the Earth in the Mesozoic Era. Like lepidosaurians, they also had a diapsid skull. The first archosaurs which appeared during the Permian period are called pseudosuchian thecodonts. The most typical pseudosuchian forms, from which dinosaurs and birds eventually evolved, did not appear until the Triassic.

The Euryapsids also appeared during the Permian period, represented by the order Protorosauria. The group contained mainly small species that had a parapsid skull (one with a single opening corresponding to the upper temporal opening in a diapsid skull). Protorosaurs were like lizards in appearance and were predators. They included *Araeoscelis*, about 30 centimetres long, and *Tridentinosaurus*, from the Permian of Italy.

The Synapsida were the most important group of Palaeozoic reptiles. The synapsid skull typically had a single temporal opening corresponding to the lower temporal opening in a diapsid skull. Synapsids are important not just because there were very many of them and they had proliferated throughout the world, but because during the late Triassic period primitive mammals evolved from them. The Synapsida were in existence from the Permian to the Jurassic periods and are divided into two orders: the Pelycosauria and Therapsida ('mammal-like' reptiles).

Pelycosaurs were exclusively Permian. The most primitive forms included two large lizards: *Ophiacodon*, two and a half metres long, and *Varanosaurus*, one and a half metres long. They had pointed teeth and this suggests they were predators. Two groups evolved from them, one with carnivorous habits, the other herbivorous. *Dimetrodon* was a typical representative of the first. It had differentiated teeth (anticipating one of the typically mammalian features) and a curious dorsal 'sail', which was formed by a membrane stretched between spines extending from the vertebrae. What purpose this crest served is a mystery, although it is generally thought that it might have been used to regulate body temperature. *Edaphosaurus* was a typical herbivorous pelycosaur. It was about three metres long, and like *Dimetrodon* it also had a dorsal crest.

Therapsid remains have been found all over the world. The skeleton shows distinct mammalian characteristics, such as differentiated teeth, and fewer bones in the skull and limbs positioned under the body. A typical Permian therapsid was *Moschops*, which was as large as a rhinoceros.

Land plants

Plants began to colonize dry land in the late Silurian, and gradually the earth became green. The characteristic flora of the Devonian, Carboniferous and Permian periods was basically made up of fern-like plants, giant versions of horsetails and various primitive conifers.

The first land plants, the psilophytales, had no true roots or leaves, but comprised simple branching stalks, with spore-bearing bodies at the tops. They grew close to rivers or lakes, and most were of small size, less than 30 centimetres high. *Rhynia* and *Asteroxylon* are two well-known genera. The first was a small plant about 20 centimetres high. The stalk was smooth and straight, carrying sporangia at the tips of the highest branches. The *Asteroxylon* stalk was covered with a large number of thorny leaflets not much more than one centimetre long. Psilophytes had become extinct by the end of the Devonian period.

The Lycopodiales (clubmosses), Equisetales (horsetails) and Filicales (ferns) appeared alongside psilophytales during the course of the Devonian period. They became so well established and successful that the first true forests were formed before the end of the period. During the Carboniferous period some parts of the world were covered with enormous forests made up of these plants, and these produced large coal deposits. Only a very few of these ancient plants have survived to the present day. The ones that have are always small, and are nothing like the impressive trees that covered the earth during the last phase of the Palaeozoic Era.

The oldest known lycopod, which was found in Devonian beds

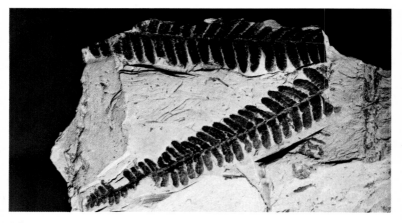

▲ *Pecopteris* leaves

in Australia, is *Baragwantia*. It was a large herbaceous form with narrow leaves several centimetres long growing out of the stalk. However most Palaeozoic lycopods were huge trees that could grow to a height of over 30 metres. They had true leaves and roots. Lycopod trees typically had a very tall trunk, at the top of which were simply forked leaf-bearing branches. At the bottom of the trunk was a complex root apparatus composed of large rhizomes – up to 10 metres long – to which the true roots were attached. These root formations are relatively common as fossils and are often found in 'life position'. All these roots have been classified as *Stigmaria*, though they must have belonged to many

▲ Fronds of the pteridosperm *Sphenopteris*

133

different kinds of lycopods. The leaves were arranged spirally round the trunk and branches and left a scar when they fell off; as every kind of lycopod had its own specific kind of leaf-scar pattern, this is useful for identification.

The most representative Carboniferous lycopods are *Lepidodendron* and *Sigillaria*. The first looked rather like the Mediterranean pine, with its branches spreading into an umbrella and carrying spore-bearing bodies at the ends. The leaf-scars are typically lozenge-shaped. *Sigillaria* leaf-scars are hexagonal and the leaves were arranged in plumes on the highest parts of the tree. The spore-bearing bodies were situated round the branches just below the tufts of leaves.

Equisetales, which were important as Carboniferous coal-formers, included tree-like as well as herbaceous forms. Both had a typically segmented trunk with leaf whorls at the base of each segment. Like lycopods, tree-like Equisetales could reach a height of 30 metres. The well-known genus *Calamites* had characteristic

▼ Fossil pteridosperm seeds from the Carboniferous

▲ Bark of *Sigillaria*

▲ Fragment of *Sigillaria* trunk

vertical flutings which alternated from one segment to the next along its trunk and branches. In discussing the Filicales mention must be made of a similar group, the Pteridosperms or seed-ferns. The two groups are so alike it is often difficult to establish to which of the two a fossil belongs. The plant can often only be classified as a pteridosperm when seeds and leaves are found together. Classification is therefore very difficult and is basically morphological, and genera and species are established according to the shape of the leaves. Palaeozoic fern leaves closely resemble those of living ferns and were particularly large in relation to the trunk. There are also known cases of tree-ferns.

By the end of the Devonian period the groups discussed above had been joined by the first Cordaitales and Coniferales. These were particularly important, since during the last phase of the Palaeozoic Era they formed large forests in mountainous areas or places that were too dry for the other groups to flourish. Cordaitales, of which *Cordaites* is a well-known genus, appeared in the Devonian period and became extinct during the Permian, and were trees 30 or 40 metres high, with branches concentrated at the top. The leaves could be one metre long and grew spirally round the branches. Coniferales, with their typical conical shape and needle-shaped leaves, probably evolved from *Cordaites* in

▼ The diagram below is a hypothetical illustration
of the various evolutionary phases
of a coastal region during Carboniferous times
and explains why fossil coal seams occur in
such even series. The green-coloured strata
in the sectioned diagram indicate
marine deposits; brown strata are lagoon deposits;
the black strata are the coal seams
that were gradually
formed on the sea bed.
1) The lagoon is formed
2) The lagoon is partially filled
3) The lagoon has disappeared beneath marshes
covered with lush vegetation
4) The sea floods the region
and buries the vegetable remains
5) Marine sediments cover the layer of
vegetable matter. Deposition of
sedimentary material by rivers will
eventually lead to the formation of a
new lagoon, re-creating the initial
conditions that will allow the cycle
to repeat itself and so form
another layer of coal.

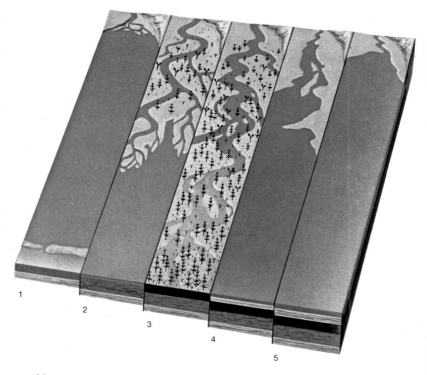

1

2

3

4

5

▲ Leaf scars on the bark of *Lepidodendron sternbergii*

Carboniferous times and during the Permian period were represented by *Lebachia* and *Ullmannia*.

The origin of coal

Large deposits of coal were formed during the Carboniferous period. Basically they were made up of Lycopodiales, Equisetales, Filicales and Cordaitales, plants that formed lush

▼ *Cordaitale* leaf

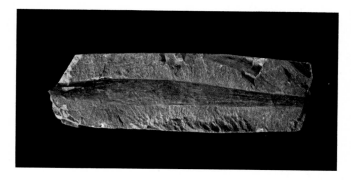

forests over large areas that now lie in the northern hemisphere.

Coal is found in seams or in very flat fields sandwiched between beds of sedimentary rock. These beds are normally of sandstone or shale. Coal seams may cover very wide areas, and their thickness varies from a few centimetres to two to three metres. Thicker seams are rare. Coal deposits often contain large numbers of seams one on top of another, separated by layers of sandstone or shale.

▲ Carboniferous forest diorama

Much research has been done into the origin of coal and the results indicate that it was formed when plant debris accumulated in vast areas covered with thick, swampy forests that were periodically flooded by the sea. The climate must have been hot and humid with high rainfall. Thick layers of vegetable matter gradually formed as the years passed. When the sea flooded the swamps the forest slowly died and the accumulated vegetation was buried beneath marine sediments. The deposition of sedimentary material quickly filled the basin again and land re-emerged. New forests grew on the virgin land and another layer of vegetable matter began to accumulate. Another flood buried this bed under more marine sediments until land reappeared and a new forest grew. The repetition of this cycle explains why coal seams occur in regular series.

Once the vegetable matter had been cut off from contact with

▲ Reconstructed habitat of a Carboniferous stegocephalous amphibian

the atmosphere, it was attacked by anaerobic bacteria. This released hydrogen, oxygen and nitrogen and so increased the proportion of carbon. Because new sediments were constantly accumulating the vegetable debris sank lower and lower and the weight of the sediments on top gradually increased. This pressure gradually compacted the plant remains, and eventually they turned into coal.

The Mesozoic Era

The name Mesozoic comes from the Greek *meson* (middle) and *zoon* (living). This refers to the fact that Mesozoic organisms were halfway between the more primitive animals and plants of the Palaeozoic Era and the more modern species that existed in the succeeding Cainozoic Era. It has been estimated that the Mesozoic Era, which has been divided into three periods, the Triassic, Jurassic and Cretaceous, lasted about 160 million years.

The beginning of the Mesozoic Era more or less coincided with the start of the Alpine mountain-building cycle, which was to continue into the next era and lead to the formation of the world's youngest mountain chains (the Alps, Apennines, Pyrenees,

Carpathians, Caucasus, Himalayas, Andes and Rockies). Major tectonic movements occurred right at the start of the era, mostly along the Pacific coasts of the American continents.

At the beginning of the Mesozoic Era, all the continents were locked together in one enormous 'supercontinent' called Pangaea, the result of the different continental masses moving together during the Palaeozoic. Pangaea began to split up at the beginning of the Jurassic period, and from that point the various continental masses slowly shifted towards the positions they occupy today, resulting in the formation of the Atlantic and Indian Oceans. A palaeogeographic map of the Mesozoic Era is on the next page.

The southern Atlantic seems to have formed in the early Cretaceous, the northern in the late Cretaceous.

The Mesozoic Era is commonly known as the 'Age of Reptiles', since these vertebrates dominated land, sea, and air for its duration. The major evolutionary events that occurred were the appearance of mammals in the late Triassic and birds in the late Jurassic. The earliest angiosperms (plants with flowers and encased seeds) are from the late Triassic period. In the Cretaceous period, angiosperms eclipsed gymnosperms (conifers) and evolved into the characteristic flora of the present day. At the end of the era a great crisis seems to have affected nearly the whole animal world and as a result a great many previously dominant groups suddenly became extinct.

Life in the sea

The underwater worlds of Mesozoic and Palaeozoic times had little in common. This was true of the flora, but more especially of the fauna. Invertebrate animals in particular showed a strong tendency towards modernization and this led to the disappearance of more primitive forms, which were gradually replaced by more modern-looking ones. Most of the groups of

▼ Palaeogeographic map of the Mesozoic Era

 areas covered by sea

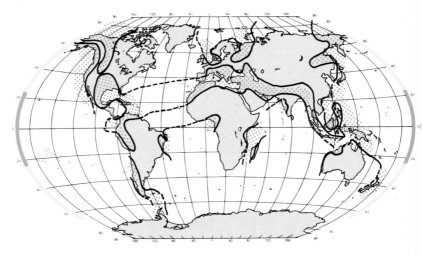

plants that had existed during the Palaeozoic seas, though, continued to flourish in Mesozoic times. Most of these were algae, and the Chlorophyta and Rhodophyta were particularly plentiful. The Chlorophyta included the Codiaceae and the Dasycladaceae, and the latter were important reef-builders during the Triassic period. The most important genera were *Gyroporella* and *Diplopora*. Solenoporacae, from which the Corallinaceae evolved during the Cretaceous period, were the most important of the Rhodophyta.

Moving on to the animal kingdom, particularly the invertebrates, the Protozoa must be mentioned first. The main groups were the Radiolaria, Foraminifera and Ciliata. From the point of view of zone fossils, Foraminifera are very important in Mesozoic rocks, just as they are in some Palaeozoic. They include large forms (Macroforaminifera), most of which had adapted to life on the sea bed, as well as microscopic forms (Microforaminifera). The first group includes the Alveolinidae, which appeared in the Cretaceous period, and the Orbitolites, which were particularly widespread in Jurassic times.

In the Microforaminifera the planktonic forms represented by *Globotruncana* and similar genera were very common from the

▼ *Plocoscyphia labrosa*, a Cretaceous sponge

beginning of the Cretaceous period onwards. The Calpionellidae were also planktonic. These microscopic protozoans belong to the Ciliata (widespread between the late Jurassic and early Cretaceous periods) and had a cup-shaped shell made of chitin and calcite (*Calpionella* is a typical genus).

Like the Protozoa, the Porifera (sponges) were widespread in Mesozoic times. Spicules (small calcareous or siliceous elements which give rigidity to a sponge) are commonly the only parts of a sponge to be fossilized. However, many complete sponge specimens are found, and *Raphidonema* (Jurassic and Cretaceous) is a common form.

▲ *Pygites diphyoides*, a Jurassic brachiopod

Coelenterates were represented mainly by hexacorals, which had replaced tetracorals at the beginning of the Triassic. They are commonly colonial and played an important part in building reef-like masses. Jellyfish, being soft-bodied, only fossilize in exceptional circumstances, but are represented by some magnificent specimens from the late Jurassic lithographic limestones of Solenhofen in Germany. Bryozoans were very important and were represented by a large number of different forms that generally inhabited shallow marine environments.

Brachiopods declined sharply during the Mesozoic, and their characteristic habitat – the continental shelf – was largely taken over by molluscs. The decline occurred mainly among the articulate brachiopods, the inarticulates maintaining similar

▲ *Thecosmilia trichotoma*, a Jurassic hexacoral

Prionorhynchia ▶
quinqueplicata,
a Jurassic brachiopod

145

▲ *Aeger insignis*, a late Jurassic lobster-like crustacean

numbers to the Palaeozoic. In addition to a general decrease in the number of articulate genera, two of the four Palaeozoic brachiopod groups that had continued into the Mesozoic, the Strophomenida and Spiriferida became extinct at the end of the

▼ *Coleia mediterranea*, an early Jurassic crustacean

Mesolimulus walchii, a Jurassic xiphosurian (king-crab) ▶

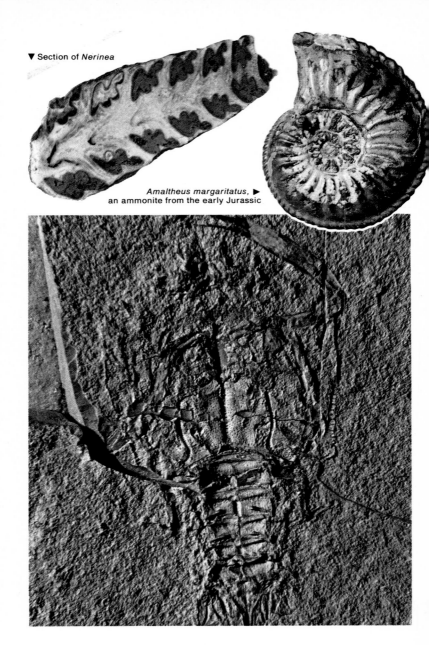

▼ Section of *Nerinea*

Amaltheus margaritatus, ▶
an ammonite from the early Jurassic

▲ *Eryon arctiformis*, a Jurassic decapod crustacean

▲ The bivalve *Lopha cristagalli*

▼ *Hippurites radians*, a late Cretaceous rudist

149

Jurassic period. The other two groups – Rhynchonellida and Terebratulida – remained fairly important, particularly during the Triassic period, and are still in existence. Characteristic genera of the Terebratulida are *Coenothyris* (Triassic), and *Pygope* and *Pygites*, both of which lived in late Jurassic times. The main genus of the Rhynchonellida that should be mentioned is *Rhynchonella* (late Jurassic). *Retzia (Tetractinella)*, an exclusively Triassic spiriferid, was also fairly important.

The only organisms of any importance in the 'worm' group are polychaete annelids, which are represented by both mobile and sessile forms during the Mesozoic. Fossil trails and burrows have been ascribed to these 'worms', among them those grouped into the 'genera' *Fucoides* and *Chondrites*. Conodonts were common until the end of the Triassic period when they became extinct. They are further discussed in the Palaeozoic chapter.

Arthropods are another invertebrate group whose marine forms were reduced in numbers in the Mesozoic fossil record. Forms adapted to living on dry land – arachnids (spiders, scorpions, etc.), myriapods (millipedes) and insects for example – became very successful. Xiphosurans had appeared during the late Palaeozoic. They are a merostome subclass, which is still in existence, and were represented by the genus *Mesolimulus*, which was widespread during the Jurassic period.

Still in the arthropod world, crustaceans were represented by a great many marine subclasses during the Mesozoic Era and

▼ *Calliphylloceras nilssoni*, a Jurassic ammonite

▼ *Ceratites nodosus*, a Triassic cephalopod

began to gain a certain amount of importance. They included branchiopods and ostracods (both of which are small crustaceans which have shells very like those of bivalves), cirripeds or barnacles, which lived (and still do) attached to rocks or other organisms near the shore.

The Mesozoic crustaceans that produced the most fossils are the decapods, which include lobsters and their allies, such as *Eryon*, *Aeger* and *Coleia*, as well as various crabs. Shrimps and prawns have a much more delicate carapace, and are therefore rarer as fossils.

Molluscs became particularly important during the Mesozoic Era. The minor groups – monoplacophorans, amphineurans and scaphopods – however, remained in small numbers only. Bivalves increased greatly in importance, and occupied many niches on the continental shelves previously occupied by brachiopods. There is a vast number of Mesozoic genera, belonging mainly to the anisomyarian and eulamellibranch groups. The first includes *Daonella* (Triassic), *Gryphaea* and *Lithiotis*, which were particularly common during the Jurassic period, and *Inoceramus*, typical of the Cretaceous period. Eulamellibranchs include *Myophoria*, which is particularly widespread in Triassic rocks, the megalodont family, which was to become very common during the late Triassic, and the rudists. Rudists adapted a conical shell and lived in colonies, and formed reefs in a similar way to corals in the Jurassic and Cretaceous periods.

▼ *Lytoceras cornucopia*, a Jurassic ammonite

▼*Euhoplites opalinus* a Cretaceous ammonite

▲ *Crioceratites emmereci*, an early Cretaceous ammonite

◄ *Turrilites*, a late Cretaceous ammonite with a turreted shell

▲ Belemnite 'guards' or rostrums (see p. 157)

Bivalves shared their habitat with gastropods (snails). The numbers of gastropods living in Mesozoic seas, however, never equalled those of bivalves. The Nerineidae should be mentioned in particular. These Jurassic and Cretaceous gastropods had a tall, turreted shell which was greatly thickened in places, possibly to protect it from buffeting by the waves.

Cephalopods are the most important molluscs and perhaps the most important invertebrates of the Mesozoic Era, just as trilobites were during the earlier part of the Palaeozoic Era. Nautiloids, ammonites and belemnites are the important groups from the palaeontological point of view. A feature common to all these cephalopods is the calcareous or aragonitic shell, which can be either external or internal. Most nautiloids and ammonites had a plano-spiral shell, and in all it is divided into chambers by means of septa, which in the ammonites gradually became more complex in the course of evolution.

Nautiloids had been very common throughout the Palaeozoic

▲ *Encrinus liliformis*, a Middle Triassic crinoid

Era, but they were much reduced in numbers in Mesozoic times. At the beginning of the Triassic period they were largely replaced by ammonites, which expanded in numbers and variety to an extraordinary degree. For reasons that are still unknown, ammonites had become extinct by the end of the Cretaceous period. Nautiloids, however, are still in existence and are represented by a small number of species belonging to the genus *Nautilus*, which looks very similar to its Mesozoic ancestors.

The ancestors of the ammonites appeared in the Palaeozoic Era, but the ammonites themselves did not appear until the Mesozoic. Ammonites are the most important zone fossils of Mesozoic rocks. Their distribution areas were enormous, while the time-span of many individual species was very short. With the increase in complexity of the septa, the suture lines – the intersections between the septa and the shell wall – also became more complex and convoluted. These are very important in the identification of ammonite species. Ammonites are

▼ *Saccocoma pectinata*, a late Jurassic stemless crinoid

▲ *Ophioderma egertoni,*
an early Jurassic brittle-star

▲ *Leptolepis knorrii,*
a late Jurassic teleost fish

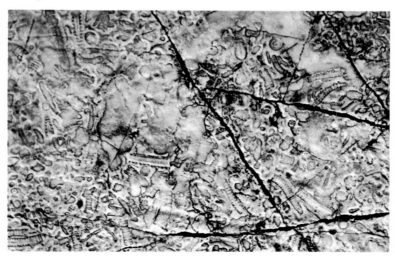

▲ Triassic dasycladeacean algae of the genus *Diplopora*

subdivided into a great many species and subspecies, and are some of the most intensively studied fossils.

Ammonites were free-swimming organisms, though the features of some groups seem to indicate that they could also live on the sea bed. When ammonites died their shell might float for a very long time (we can still see this in the case of *Nautilus*) and so they might be carried long distances by ocean currents into habitats that were different from those they had occupied in life.

Belemnites were also important during the Mesozoic Era and became extinct at the end of the Cretaceous period. The part that generally became fossilized was their calcareous 'guard' or rostrum, which in some respects is like the internal shell of a cuttle-fish, but rather more complex. The many genera of belemnites include *Atractites*, which was common from the Triassic to the Jurassic periods, *Duvalia* (late Jurassic and early Cretaceous) and *Belemnitella* (early Cretaceous).

The history of well-known living cephalopods such as cuttle-fish, squid and octopus, extends back into the Mesozoic Era, but they are rarely preserved as fossils.

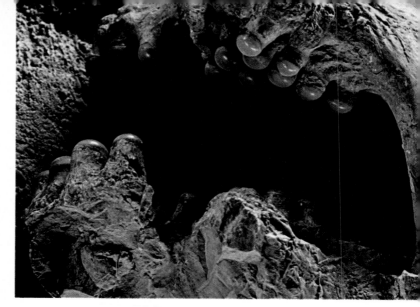

▼ ▲ Top: palatal teeth of *Lepidotus*, a Jurassic-Cretaceous fish;
bottom: a complete specimen

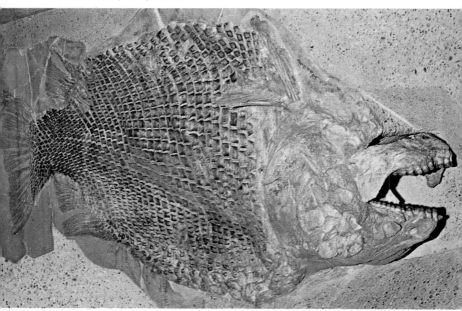

Crushing teeth of *Ptychodus*, ▶
a Cretaceous shark

The echinoderms are represented by classes that still exist today, such as crinoids, starfish, holothurians and echinoids or sea-urchins. Crinoids, which include a great many genera such as *Encrinus*, *Dadocrinus* and *Pentacrinus*, were very abundant in coastal waters, particularly in the Triassic and Jurassic periods. The late Jurassic genus *Saccocoma* was a free-swimming crinoid, which had lost its stalk.

The starfish group, represented by brittle-stars and true starfish, were less common however, as were the holothurians. Echinoids, which were represented by both regular and irregular forms very similar to those living now, were common and widespread. Regular echinoids include *Cidaris* and *Pseudodiadema*, which have been found in rocks of the whole Mesozoic Era; irregular echinoids include *Stenonaster*, *Ananchytes* and *Micraster*, which were particularly common during the Cretaceous period, and *Micraster* is important as a zone fossil in chalk.

Before going on to vertebrates mention must be made of the closely related hermichordates, such as the marine protochordate pterobranch genera *Cephalodiscus* and *Rhabdopleura*, both of which are represented (though uncommonly) in the Mesozoic.

Fishes were the most common marine vertebrates during the Mesozoic Era, and two groups, the chondrichthyans and osteichthyans, are commonly represented by fossils. Chondrichthyans are represented by two genera of selachians (modern sharks), *Isurus* and *Charcharodon*, two genera of batoideans that appeared during the Jurassic, the ray-like *Ptychodus* and *Myliobatis*, and holocephalians, which include the modern chimaera. Chondrichthyans, whose fossil remains are mostly teeth, expanded considerably from the beginning of the Cretaceous period onwards.

Actinopterygians were very important members of the osteichthyian group, and were represented by teleosts, bony fishes that appeared during the Jurassic period and very quickly spread

▼ Perfectly preserved skeleton of *Askeptosaurus italicus*, a Triassic reptile

into every ocean and river. The oldest marine representative of the group is *Leptolepis*. Other actinopterygian groups, which had already appeared during the Palaeozoic Era, or in the Triassic, only adapted to freshwater life. Crossopterygians are also important osteichthyians and this group includes coelacanths, which were believed to have become extinct during the Cretaceous period, until several living coelacanth specimens were found in the Indian Ocean in the late 1930s.

During the Mesozoic Era no amphibian seems to have adapted to living in a marine environment, but remained associated with freshwater environments. On the other hand, there were large

▲ Skeleton of *Plesiosaurus macrocephalus*

numbers of reptiles living in the sea. Indeed some should be regarded as true marine animals. Many of the classes into which reptiles are divided are represented, demonstrating the great adaptive capabilities these animals possessed during the Mesozoic Era when they were at the peak of their development. The anapsids included the chelonians, which were widespread from the beginning of the Triassic period onwards and were represented by forms adapted to various environments. The marine genus *Protostega*, which lived during the Cretaceous period, was particularly important.

The reptiles that were best adapted to marine life were the ichthyopterygians. In some respects these creatures were like dolphins, but they were often much longer. One ichthyopterygian group – the mixosaurs – was exclusively Triassic. True

▼ Skeleton of *Stenopterygius quadriscissus*, a Jurassic ichthyosaur

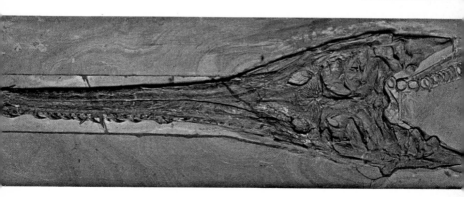

▲ Skull of *Mystriosaurus bollensis*, a marine crocodile
163

ichthyosaurs were very common during Jurassic and Cretaceous times, and some magnificent specimens have been found at Holzmaden in Germany. Their hydrodynamic shape, pointed nose and powerful tail, which enabled them to move very fast, made them better able to live in the open sea than any other reptile. They had a large number of conical teeth in a very long muzzle, and the limbs had become paired fins which acted as stabilizers.

The lepidosaurian reptile group included *Askeptosaurus*, a Triassic eosuchian that could be as long as two metres and the mosasaurs, enormous marine lizards of the Cretaceous period that seem to have fed mainly on ammonites.

▲ *Cryptocleidus oxoniensis*, a late Jurassic plesiosaur

Archosaur reptiles, in particular crocodilians, also included a typically marine group – the mesosuchians. The group's most representative genus, which appeared in the Jurassic period, was *Mystriosaurus*.

Euryapsids were the largest group of marine reptiles, or at least those that could live partly in the sea. Many of them were

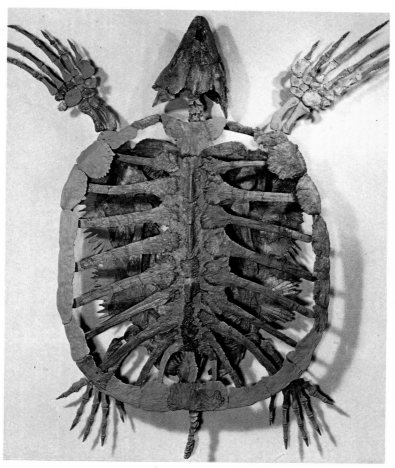

▲ *Protostega gigas*, a Cretaceous marine chelonian (turtle)

exclusively Triassic and these were the protorosaurs, which were represented by *Tanystropheus*, nothosaurs, which included small reptiles such as *Lariosaurus* and *Ceresiosaurus*, and placodonts. The name placodont comes from the reptiles' characteristic flat teeth, which were adapted to a diet of shelled animals. Placodonts had a thickset body and there was sometimes a strong protective shell over their back. Their limbs were not very specialized, which suggests that although they spent part of their time in offshore waters, they were also capable of moving about on dry land. Nothosaurs probably also had amphibian characteristics, since their limbs were barely specialized. Compared with placodonts, however, they had a more streamlined body and a longer neck and tail.

The plesiosaurs are the most well-known marine euryapsids, which lived from the end of the Triassic until the end of the

▲ Skeleton of *Ceresiosaurus calcagnii*, a Triassic nothosaur

Cretaceous period. They were very large animals, sometimes as long as 13 metres and were completely adapted to an aquatic life. Their limbs had become modified as swimming paddles and the animals used them as a means of propulsion. Characteristic genera are *Plesiosaurus*, which was three metres long, and *Elasmosaurus*, which could be anything up to 13 metres long. In spite of the great number of different forms, the euryapsids never became as perfectly adapted to living in the sea as the ichthyosaurs.

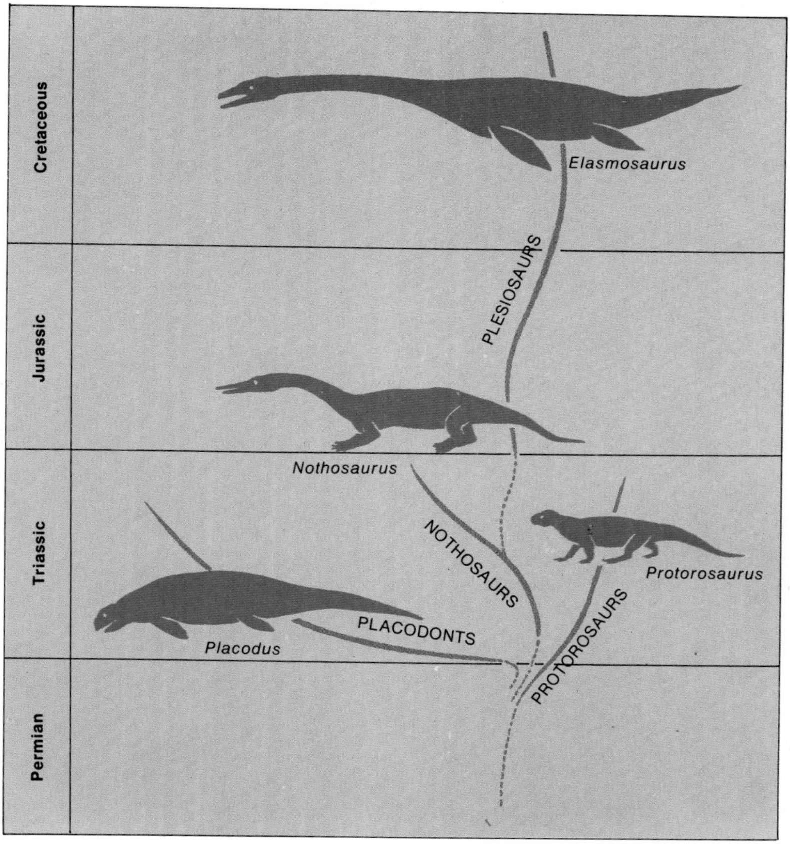
Cretaceous
Jurassic
Triassic
Permian
Elasmosaurus
PLESIOSAURS
Nothosaurus
NOTHOSAURS
Protorosaurus
PROTOROSAURS
PLACODONTS
Placodus

▲ Evolution of Euryapsid reptiles

Reptile domination

It has already been said that the Mesozoic Era is also known as the 'Age of Reptiles' because during its 160 million years, reptiles had control of land, sea and air. They had evolved from an amphibian group, the Embolomeri, and appeared in the Middle Carboniferous period. It can be said that amphibians were responsible for their own destruction, in view of the extent to which reptiles had quickly spread and differentiated before the Palaeozoic Era was over, with the resulting sharp drop in the amphibian population. Amphibians were unable to hold out against the strong competition presented by animals that were so much more evolved, adapted and practical. But reptilian evolution during the Palaeozoic Era was insignificant compared with the overwhelming supremacy they achieved in Mesozoic times.

Anapsid cotylosaurs were the most primitive reptiles and all subsequent forms evolved from them. Cotylosaurs were mostly Carboniferous and Permian and only one group survived into the Triassic before becoming extinct. But another group that also evolved from the anapsids, the chelonians, have survived to the present day. The first true chelonians appeared in the Triassic period, and huge specimens more than three metres long have been found in rocks dating from the Mesozoic Era.

▲ Skeletons of *Coelophysis*, Triassic thecodonts

Most reptiles still living today belong to the lepidosaurian group. Eosuchian lepidosaurs, which had appeared in the Permian period, continued into Triassic times and included forms that were well adapted to living in the sea as well as those that lived on land. *Macrocnemus* was an important representative of the second group. It was a small reptile with a long neck and slender, agile feet.

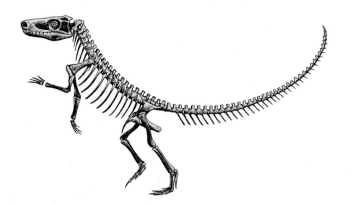

▲ *Euparkeria*, a Triassic pseudosuchian

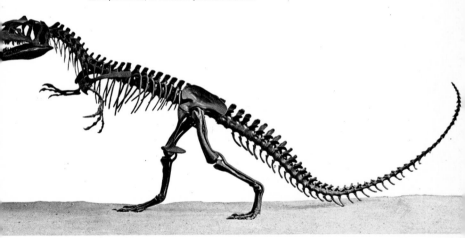

▲ *Allosaurus*, a late Jurassic carnivorous dinosaur

Lizards were much more specialized however. The lizard's diapsid skull no longer had a bar below the lower temporal opening and this enabled the reptile to move its lower jaw freely. A feature present in some modern 'flying' lizards has also been found in certain fossil specimens from the Triassic period – extremely long ribs which jutted out at either side and supported a membrane. The lizards were able to use these 'wings' to fly short distances by gliding from tree branches. Snakes, the largest of the living reptile groups, probably evolved from lizards in the Cretaceous period. The main modifications in this most recent lepidosaurian group were the loss of limbs and the ability to open the mouth very wide to swallow prey larger than themselves.

The real rulers of the Mesozoic world were archosaurs, among which are the largest land carnivores that have ever existed. Crocodiles and their allies are now the only survivors of this group. An important archosaur characteristic is that many adopted the bipedal habit – walking on two legs.

Thecodonts were among the most primitive archosaurs. They appeared in the Permian period and were represented by pseudosuchians, which were characteristically bipedal. *Euparkeria*, which was just under one metre long, is a typical Triassic representative of this group. The enormous size of the hind legs compared with the front legs as well as its long, powerful tail suggest that it was an animal that had adapted to running on two legs and that it could move remarkably fast. It is worth emphasizing that all other archosaur groups – dinosaurs in particular – evolved from pseudosuchians like *Euparkeria*. The ancestry of the birds is probably among primitive thecodonts.

There were other thecodonts living alongside pseudosuchians in Triassic times, the phytosaurs and aetosaurs, and they were quadruped and similar to crocodiles in appearance and in their life habits. They had no direct evolutionary link with crocodilians, however, apart from belonging to the archosaur group. Crocodiles, which also appeared in the Triassic period, seem to have reached a more advanced stage in their evolution. One of the features which distinguishes them from phytosaurs is a secondary palate that stops water entering their respiratory tracts when they open their mouthes under water. A great many genera can be included among crocodilians, some of which were adapted to living in the sea, for example *Mystriosaurus*. *Protosuchus*, which was just under one metre long and had bony scales over its body, was one of the first crocodilians. *Deinosuchus*, from the late Cretaceous, was the largest crocodile that has ever existed, being at least 15 metres long.

Dinosaurs were the most important of the archosaur groups, at least as far as numbers went. It must be pointed out that the term 'dinosaur' ('terrible lizard') has no taxonomic value, since it includes two very different orders – the saurischians and the ornithischians. These two groups are classified according to the shape and arrangement of their pelvic bones. In saurischians the pubis bone is tilted forward, whereas in ornithischians it is tilted backwards and in addition is joined to the ischium bone.

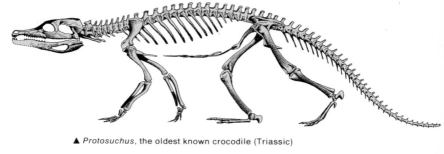

▲ *Protosuchus*, the oldest known crocodile (Triassic)

Dinosaurs did not all have the same habits. Some saurischians were bipedal and carnivorous, while others were quadruped and herbivorous. Ornithischians were all herbivorous, and there were both bipedal and quadruped forms.

The first dinosaurs appeared in the Triassic period and belonged to the saurischian group. Some were very small, but

▼ Reconstruction of *Rutidion*, a Triassic phytosaur

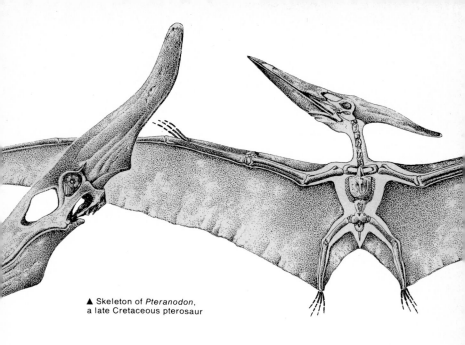

▲ Skeleton of *Pteranodon*,
a late Cretaceous pterosaur

others were much larger, five to six metres long. They were bipedal, and the weight of the body was balanced by a long, powerful tail. When it was resting the animal therefore had three firm areas of support.

Saurischians are divided into two suborders. The theropod group covers the carnivorous, bipedal forms, and includes a great many genera of various different sizes. While some were no larger than dogs, others were enormous. *Antrodemus* from the Triassic was about nine metres long. Its front limbs, armed with powerful claws, were very small, and it had a set of sharp teeth. *Allosaurus* and *Tyrannosaurus* had similar characteristics. *Tyrannosaurus* was 14 metres long – its head alone was more than one metre – and it stood about six metres high. Its weight has been estimated at almost seven tonnes. It was therefore the largest carnivore in the world. The limbs had four toes armed with claws (on the hind limbs three toes faced forwards and one faced backwards (as in birds). The front limbs were so small that it is difficult to imagine what they could have been used for, except perhaps for clasping food while it was being eaten.

Sauropods formed the second saurischian group. They were quadruped herbivores, and included the largest land animals that have ever existed. The body was generally short and stood on

◀ Reconstruction of the habitat in which pterosaurs probably lived

▲ *Pterodactylus antiquus*, a late Jurassic pterosaur
▼ *Rhamphorhynchus phyllurus*, a Jurassic pterosaur

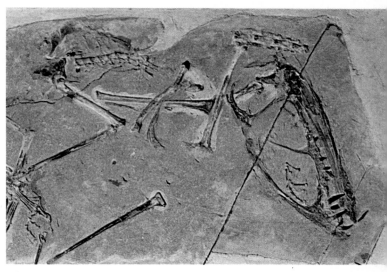

▲ *Dimorphodon*, one of the oldest known pterosaurs

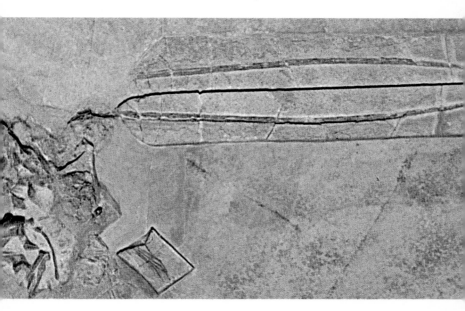

Overleaf: skeleton of *Diplodocus carnegiei*, ▶
an enormous late Jurassic sauropod

strong, column-like limbs (the fore limbs were almost always slightly shorter), and they had a very long neck and tail, a small head and weak teeth. Typical sauropods include *Brontosaurus*, which was 20 metres long and weighed about 30 tonnes, and *Diplodocus*, which was up to 27 metres long. Both lived during the late Jurassic period.

Brachiosaurus does not quite fit into the same pattern. It was 22 metres long, standing six metres high at the shoulder, and its front limbs were longer than its hind limbs. Although it was slightly shorter than other sauropods, *Brachiosaurus* was much heavier and bulkier. It has been calculated that the weight of the largest complete specimen was almost 80 tonnes, a figure that has only been exceeded by the blue whale. Individual *Brachiosaurus* bones have been found, however, which are much larger than their counterparts in complete skeletons, which means that some specimens might have weighed even more. *Brachiosaurus* must therefore be considered as the largest land animal and perhaps the largest creature that has ever existed on Earth.

The enormous bulk of the sauropods has raised many

▼ Reconstruction of *Stegosaurus*, a herbivorous dinosaur

questions concerning mechanical problems of these animals. The skeleton appears to be very strong, even though the presence of a great many cavities considerably reduces its weight.

Nevertheless, it must have taken a great deal of muscular strength to support and shift such a mass. It is possible that sauropods lived half-immersed in lakes and rivers, with the water helping to support the huge body weight.

A nother problem that still has to be solved concerns food. Judging by their teeth, sauropods were undoubtedly herbivores, and it must have been necessary to consume vast quantities of vegetable matter to support such a massive body. Connected with the small size of the head is the animal's remarkably tiny brain, which was so small that the spinal cord at the root of the tail was larger than the brain itself. This might have enabled the animal to co-ordinate the movements throughout the body better.

Ornithischians are the second major group into which dinosaurs are divided. This group shows a strong tendency towards walking on two legs. The bipedal forms are grouped into the ornithopod suborder, which is the most important

ornithischian lineage. *Iguanodon*, from the early Cretaceous, is the best known ornithopod. It could be as much as nine metres long and five metres high. The hind legs were extremely large compared with the front. At least 17 *Iguanodon* skeletons were once found together near the Belgian town of Bernissart. This association suggests that these ornithopods were gregarious.

Another typical ornithopod is *Camptosaurus*, which lived in the late Jurassic and early Cretaceous periods. It had stumpy hind legs, and its front legs were larger compared with those of *Iguanodon*. Its overall size was also smaller. The shape of the limbs and the structure of the whole skeleton suggest that it might have been a swamp-dwelling animal.

Some ornithopods of the late Cretaceous period developed very strange features. They broadly resembled iguanodons, but they had a 'beak' on the front of the long, flat skull. It resembles a duck's bill, hence their name, 'duck-billed dinosaurs'. The teeth were confined to the back of the mouth and there were large numbers of them. The mummified meal that was found in the stomach of one of these reptiles shows that their basic food was conifer needles, fruits and seeds. Some 'duck-billed dinosaurs' (also known as hadrosaurs) had in addition a strange bony head crest pierced by long, sinuous nasal tubes. The function of these is a mystery.

Three groups evolved from ornithopods during the Jurassic and Cretaceous periods. Although they kept the basic ornithischian characteristics, they differed a great deal from the parent group. The Jurassic and Cretaceous stegosaurs were quadrupeds up to six metres long. They had shorter front limbs, which meant that their head was brought fairly close to the ground. The most striking characteristic of this well-known group is the two lines of large bony plates along the back. Ankylosaurs were exclusively Cretaceous. They were protected by bony plates that made them look like an armadillo. Some ankylosaurs also had strong spikes on the tail and along the sides of the plate-covered body.

Ceratopsians are the last ornithischian group still to be discussed. They were the last dinosaurs to evolve and did not appear until towards the end of the Cretaceous period. Ceratopsians are also known as 'horned dinosaurs' because they had one, two or even three horns on their head. Compared with the rest of the body, the head could sometimes be very large, as much as one-third of the animal's total length. The back of the head broadened out into a bony collar that probably acted as protection as well as an attachment for the powerful neck and jaw muscles. The front of the head ended in a 'beak'.

◀ Reconstruction of *Iguanodon bernissartensis*, an early Cretaceous ornithopod

Primitive ceratopsians, for example *Protoceratops*, were small, no more than two metres long, and had no horns. In the more evolved types we see a considerable increase in size (up to eight metres in length) a wider bony collar and horn development. *Monoclonius* is a typical example of a one-horned ceratopsian, and *Triceratops* is a typical three-horned specimen, with one horn on the end of the snout and two on the top of the head.

Adaptation to flight was among the archosaurs' most incredible acquisitions. Flying reptiles, or pterosaurs, existed from the beginning of the Jurassic period to the end of the Cretaceous. The wing was formed by a membrane stretched over the front limb and its extremely elongated fourth digit. Compared with the body, the head was very large. The muscles responsible for moving the wings do not seem to have been very powerful, since the breast-bone was not as large as it is in birds. The toes were clawed, and their structure suggests that pterosaurs were unable to walk on their hind limbs. They presumably used them to

▼ Skeletons of *Protoceratops*, late Cretaceous ceratopsians

perch on trees or rocks or at best to drag themselves along the ground. They were probably able to glide from heights on air currents, rather than fly like true birds.

The most primitive pterosaur was *Dimorphodon*, which had an enormous head and a very long tail. The end of the tail of *Rhamphorhynchus* was broadened like a paddle, and probably acted as a rudder. These two genera were usually small – the wing span was one metre wide at the most. *Pterodactylus*, which did not have a tail, was also small, being not much larger than a pigeon. *Pteranodon*, however, from the late Cretaceous, was enormous – its wing span was almost 10 metres wide. It had no teeth but a long beak, and this was counterbalanced by the elongation at the back of the skull.

Through their many evolutionary modifications reptiles produced something that was basically new and more advanced in the long history of evolution – mammals. The vertebrates that would dominate the Earth during the Cainozoic Era evolved from a group of sinapsid reptiles that had appeared in the Permian period and survived into the Jurassic. These reptiles are called therapsids or mammal-like reptiles and they possessed some typically mammalian features in their skeleton such as

▼ Skeleton of *Triceratops*, a late Cretaceous ceratopsian

183

▲ Skeleton of *Tyrannosaurus*, a Cretaceous theropod

▼ Reconstruction of *Ankylosaurus*, a Cretaceous ornithischian dinosaur

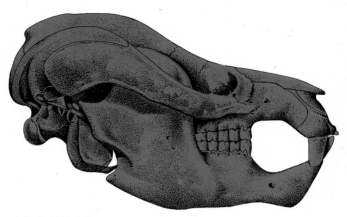

▲ Skull of *Tritylodon*, a late Triassic mammal-like reptile

differentiated teeth, a gradual increase in the number of bones in the skull, particularly those of the lower jaw, and a tendency for the limbs to extend from the sides of the body rather than being positioned under it. Mesozoic therapsids include *Cynognathus*, a carnivore the size of a large dog, *Dicynodon*, which had no teeth but a beak, and *Tritylodon*, perhaps a transitional form between reptiles and mammals.

Primitive mammals

We cannot be sure at which point in geological time the first true mammals appeared on the Earth, but fossils indicate that in Permian and Triassic times there were reptiles so like mammals that it is sometimes difficult to establish if a skeleton is reptilian or mammalian. The oldest fossils which can definitely be said to belong to a mammal, in spite of being incomplete, are from rocks of late Triassic age. Evolution of mammals from reptiles was gradual, and all the transitional stages are not known.

The difficulty in identifying the earliest mammals stems from the fact that many of their characteristic features could not fossilize. We do not know if they were covered with fur, if they could regulate their internal body temperature, if they were viviparous (bearing living young rather than laying eggs) and so on. Palaeontological remarks must therefore be based on the study of skeletal characters alone.

Primitive mammals were very small animals, no larger than a large mouse, which they also resembled in appearance. All the

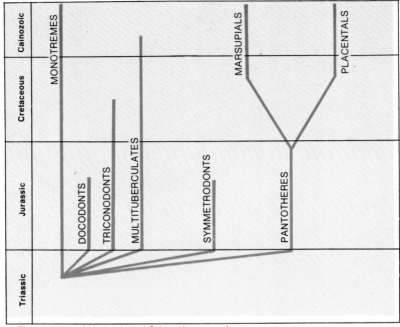

▲ The evolution of Mesozoic and Cainozoic mammals

mammals of the Mesozoic Era were small, and judging by the number of fossils that have been found they were also relatively common. Mammals were unable to spread widely until the beginning of the Cainozoic Era, when many new ecological niches appeared with the disappearance of most of the reptiles.

Primitive mammals are classified according to the shape of their teeth, since these are the most common fossils, and names of many orders refers to the tooth shape. The distinctive groups are docodonts, triconodonts, multituberculates, symmetrodonts and pantotheres.

Docodonts are the most primitive. Triconodonts, whose teeth had three conical cusps, as their name indicates, were more evolved although they still had very primitive characteristics. They include *Morganucodon* from the late Triassic of South Wales. Multituberculates, which had adapted to a herbivorous diet, are better known. They characteristically had large incisors and molars with longitudinal rows of cusps. Multituberculates

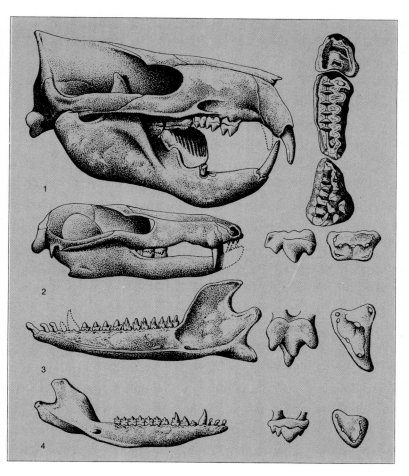

▲ Fossils belonging to the oldest known mammals: 1. skull and teeth of a multituberculate; 2. skull and teeth of a triconodont; 3. lower jaw and teeth of a pantothere; 4. lower jaw and teeth of a symmetrodont

survived longer than any other group of primitive mammals, and are known from Jurassic to Eocene times. Symmetrodonts were very probably carnivorous. Their teeth were triangular and had three very large jutting cusps.

All the groups mentioned so far seem to have left no descendants among living mammals. Pantotheres, however, the last of the primitive mammalian orders, gave rise to marsupials and placentals more or less at the same time between the end of the Jurassic and the beginning of the Cretaceous periods. Pantotheres are therefore regarded as one of the most important fossil mammal groups since they are the direct ancestors of modern mammals. Moving into the areas vacated by the large reptiles, marsupials (the young, ill-developed at birth are carried and fed in a pouch for several weeks to develop further) were at first more common than placentals (the embryo develops to an advanced stage before birth), which were represented only by insectivores (small insect-feeders). However, at the beginning of the Cainozoic Era these insectivores gave rise to other placentals, which were in time to become dominant over the marsupials.

The conquest of the air

In spite of their common parentage (they had both evolved from thecodonts) birds and pterosaurs solved the problem of flight in very different ways, and this difference was perhaps the reason why pterosaurs declined and birds were successful. Whereas pterosaurs could use their wings for little more than gliding on air currents, birds were able to achieve true flight, freed from the limitations and dangers to which flying reptiles were subject.

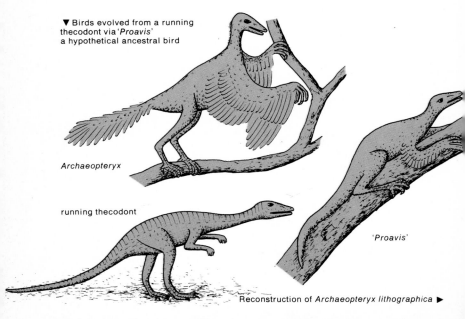

▼ Birds evolved from a running thecodont via 'Proavis' a hypothetical ancestral bird

Archaeopteryx

running thecodont

'Proavis'

Reconstruction of Archaeopteryx lithographica ▶

The skeletal features of the ancestral bird *Archaeopteryx* were definitely reptilian. It was under 50 centimetres long and had a large number of teeth. The bones lacked air-cavities to lighten them (in contrast to modern birds), the front limbs had long claws and it had a long tail with feathers at both sides. These characteristics are primitive and for the most part reptilian, showing that this winged creature was still a long way from a true bird. No other information about the primitive birds of the Jurassic period is available, although palaeontologists have tried to reconstruct a hypothetical transitional stage from an ancestor belonging to the thecodont archosaur group of reptiles. This is a reptile which walked on two legs, was possibly a fast runner and had its body covered with elongated, serrated scales that would eventually become feathers. This hypothetical ancestor probably lived in trees, and may also have been able to move by hopping from branch to branch (see page 50).

Reconstruction of *Ichthyornis*, a late Cretaceous bird ▼

There are only a few fossil birds from the Cretaceous. In spite of this, the few more or less complete specimens that have been found show the enormous progress birds had made between the end of the Jurassic and the end of the Cretaceous periods. Apart from a few isolated bones dating from the early Cretaceous period, there are two well-documented genera from the late Cretaceous – *Hesperornis* and *Ichthyornis*. The first, which was about one metre long, had legs that were perfectly adapted to swimming, although its wings were too small to be of any use for flying. Its beak was still primitive, and contained a lot of teeth. The gull-like *Ichthyornis*, which was barely 20 centimetres long, was a good flyer and had all the requirements of a true bird.

Mesozoic flora

The Mesozoic was a crucial period in the evolution of land plants. The beginning of the era coincided with a sharp decline of the

▼ Reconstruction of *Williamsonia sewardiana*   ▼ Fossilized cycad fruit

▲ Twig of *Voltzia*,
a Triassic conifer

▲ Reconstruction of *Palaeocycas
integer*, a cycad

▼ Cretaceous angiosperms: from the left, *Laurus proteaefolia*,
Aralia saporteana, *Liriophyllum populoides*

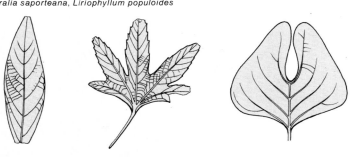

pteridophytes, the most important plants of the Palaeozoic Era, which were replaced by the rapidly expanding spermatophytes (higher plants possessing seeds and flowers). At first gymnosperms were more common, but during the Cretaceous period they were superseded by angiosperms, a more specialized group of plants and the dominant forms today.

Of the pteridophytes, only the ferns remained moderately widespread during the Mesozoic while many lycopods and equisetales became extinct early in the era. A few herbaceous members of these groups have survived in some distinct habitats down to the present day.

Between the Triassic and Jurassic periods the gymnosperms spread throughout the world. Triassic gymnosperms include several very important groups, among them the Caytoniales and pteridosperms represented by the genus *Thinnfeldia*, which should be regarded as the oldest spermatophyte. Caytoniales, *Caytonia* among them, had female reproductive organs containing structures that were like ovaries. These two primitive groups of gymnosperms declined rapidly in importance during the Mesozoic, but the cycads expanded greatly, reaching the peak of their development in the Triassic period. The most common genus was *Paleocycas*. Cycads are still in existence, although the number of genera is smaller. Bennettitales, had true flowers and included a great many characteristic genera such as *Williamsonia*, *Cycadeoidea* and many others, but became extinct during the Cretaceous period. They are an important group, since angiosperms probably evolved from them.

Between the Triassic and Jurassic periods the Ginkgoales were also very common. They are now represented by only one species, *Ginkgo biloba*. Conifers were, and still are, by far the most important of the gymnosperms. In the Triassic and Jurassic periods they were represented by many genera, for example *Voltzia*, *Araucaria*, and *Sequoia*, some of which still exist.

There are many questions surrounding the origin of the angiosperms, which appeared in the late Triassic. By the Cretaceous they had totally eclipsed all other plants. The first angiosperms possibly belonged to the monocotyledon group which included *Sanmiguelia lewisi* in the late Triassic. The first dicotyledons had appeared by the Cretaceous period and they were represented by many genera, some of which still exist, for example *Salix* (*willow*), *Laurus* (*laurel*) and *Populus* (*poplar*). The majority of modern families, both monocotyledons (such as grasses and palms) as well as dicotyledons had become established by the late Cretaceous, and by the end of the Cretaceous the modern landscape had taken shape.

The mass extinctions

The end of the Mesozoic is characterized by the total disappearance of many large animal groups that had flourished during the era. Among marine invertebrates the rudist bivalves, ammonites and belemnites all became extinct. Among the vertebrates all the dinosaurs and large marine reptiles became extinct. Only a few reptile groups, such as chelonians, squamates, rhynchocephalians and crocodilians, survived the end of the era, and are still in existence today, although in insignificant numbers compared with the enormous populations that had characterized the Mesozoic Era. Clearly it is difficult to explain the more or less simultaneous extinction of such diverse groups as the rudists, ammonites and the large reptiles. Even if these groups had reached their maximum specialization, the fact that they became

▼ Dinosaur vertebrae

▲ Valve of the rudist *Hippurites*   ▲ *Turrilites*, a Cretaceous ammonite

totally extinct so quickly, seems absolutely incomprehensible.

Many theories have been put forward to explain this, none of them entirely satisfactory. Some Cretaceous ammonite genera developed peculiar shells, which were sometimes U-shaped, as in *Hamites*, straight, as in *Baculites*, spiral, as in *Turrilites*, or completely irregular, as in *Nipponites*. This phenomenon might have something to do with the group's imminent extinction, but it is impossible to say any more than this. Until the end of their existence the ammonites were still able to display strong evolutionary potential, as shown by the emergence of a great many irregular shell forms just before the group became extinct.

A great many theories have been put forward to explain why the dinosaurs and other large reptiles became extinct, although some of them are so far-fetched that they are not worth considering seriously. There has still not been a likely explanation of this phenomenon, which obviously must be connected with a series of factors that were present at the same time in the late Cretaceous period. These might include a general change in the climate (possibly connected with mountain-building phenomena) that affected the whole world. This event may have had a strong impact on such cold-blooded creatures as reptiles. Examination of dinosaur eggs from the late Cretaceous has shown pathological irregularities in shell thickness, a possible result of a sudden cooling of the climate. The effects of such a change would doubtless be greatly felt all over the world, which up to that time had been characterized by relatively stable climatic conditions, but it does not explain the phenomenon adequately since not all reptiles became extinct.

The Cainozoic Era

The Cainozoic is the last era in the geological column. The term Cainozoic comes from the Greek *cainon* (recent) and *zoon* (living) reflecting the close resemblance of many of its fossils to present-day life. The Cainozoic Era began about 67 million years ago. It is divided into the Tertiary and Quaternary. The former is divided into five epochs – Palaeocene, Eocene, Oligocene, Miocene, and Pliocene; the latter, representing the last two million years of Earth history, is divided into Pleistocene and Holocene (or Recent). The Quaternary will be dealt with in the next chapter.

The Alpine mountain-building cycle, which had begun in the Mesozoic, continued into the Cainozoic, when it reached its final

stages. The greatest activity occurred in the middle of the era, when the world's youngest mountain ranges such as the Alps, Pyrenees, Carpathians and Himalayas were formed. Major tectonic movements continued along the American cordilleras. The continents and oceans gradually changed as these mountains were being formed, and slowly took up their present disposition.

The splitting up of Pangaea also continued into the Cainozoic Era. During the Oligocene epoch the areas of land connecting northern America and Europe finally separated and the Indian sub-continent 'collided' with the rest of Asia. In the Miocene, the Mediterranean became a large lake when access to the Atlantic

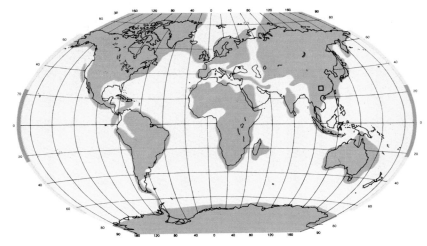

▲ Distribution of land and sea during the Cainozoic Era
(land is shown in green)

was closed; the Strait of Gibraltar was formed in Pliocene times.
In Pliocene times in America, volcanic eruptions led to the
formation of the isthmus of Panama, which joined the two
Americas together and made it possible for fauna to migrate on a
large scale. Southern Europe lay in the tropics during Palaeocene
times, but from the beginning of the Miocene there were clear
signs that the climate was starting to cool.

The Cainozoic Era has been described as the 'Age of
Mammals'. In fact, once the large reptiles had disappeared at the
end of the Cretaceous period, mammals were able to spread
throughout the world, growing in numbers, diversifying and
moving into the sea as well as the air. The group of mammals
which includes Man, the primates, first appeared in Palaeocene
times.

Life in the sea

The plants and animals living in the sea when the Cainozoic Era
began were very similar to living forms. These similarities enable
scientists to make extremely accurate palaeogeographic and
palaeoecological reconstructions, since they can back them up
with direct comparisons.

▲ The crustacean *Palinurus desmaresti*

Cainozoic marine plants include microscopic forms that make up living phytoplankton, and these are very important for zoning these rocks. Diatoms and the various groups of algae were also very widespread. Rhodophyta were particularly important algae, and one group, the Corallinaceae, were important rock-formers. The most important genera of the Rhodophyta were *Lithothamnium* and *Lithophyllum*.

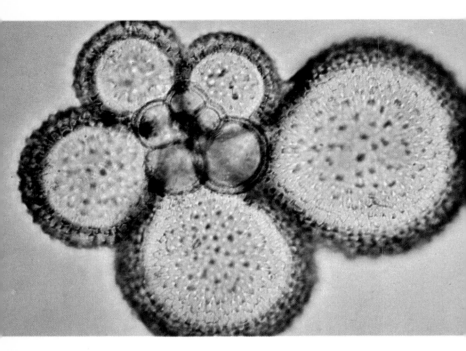

Shells of *Globigerina*, a planktonic microforaminifer ▲

◄ The Eocene macroforaminifer *Assilina*

The Protozoa include radiolarians, flagellates, and foraminifers. The latter were very important throughout the whole era and are important zone fossils. The most important foraminiferan group from this point of view were Microforaminifera, especially the planktonic ones, which are to a large extent represented by many living genera. The numbers of Macroforaminifera groups, many of which are now extinct, increased right from the start of the era. These groups included the nummulites, which had a lenticular calcareous shell containing a complex internal structure. The nummulites, represented by the genera *Nummulites*, *Assilina* and *Operculina*, were bottom-dwelling animals. Of the three genera mentioned, which we. e characteristic of the early periods of the era, only *Operculina* is still in existence, found in the Red Sea and in the seas around Japan.

Other important Macroforaminifera include the Alveolinidae (which were almost identical to Palaeozoic fusulinids) and the Orbitolites, which were disc shaped. Alveolinidae appeared in the Cretaceous period and are still in existence. The orbitolites, which included such genera as *Discocyclina*, *Lepidocyclina* and *Miogypsina*, were particularly plentiful from the late Cretaceous to mid-Miocene times.

▼ Thin section of nummulitic limestone

Cainozoic seas were also inhabited by large numbers of sponges, and apart from their characteristic spicule remains, complete sponge specimens are also commonly found in the rocks of this period. Although jellyfish and their allies were relatively important, corals, particularly the hexacorals, became much more significant during the Cainozoic Era.

Many genera, among them *Meandrina*, *Madrepora* and *Thamnastraea*, helped to build enormous reefs. Others such as *Flabellum* and *Trochosmilia* were isolated forms, however. Like the corals, the bryozoans were also very common animals in the Cainozoic seas, and were represented by a large number of genera, such as *Cellepora*, *Retepora* and *Lunulites*.

As far as brachiopods are concerned, the sharp decline that had begun at the end of the Palaeozoic Era continued during Cainozoic times. The only two groups of articulate brachiopods that were still in existence at the end of the Mesozoic Era, the

▼ The colonial coral *Meandrina*   ▼ Meandriform coral colony

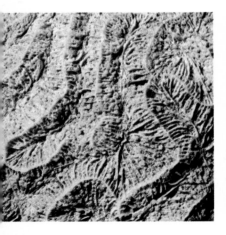 

Rhynchonellida and Terebratulida, gradually declined and there were progressively fewer genera and species living in the seas. Inarticulate brachiopod numbers remained almost the same.

Minor 'worm' groups such as the Nemertines, Nematomorpha, Nematodes, Chaetognatha and Sipunculoidea have left few fossil remains, but annelids, particularly sessile polychaete annelids, deserve special mention. Apart from a great many polychaete burrow and trail fossils there are also several genera such as *Tubulostium* and *Serpula*, which had a small calcareous tube that readily fossilized. Marine arthropods were represented by merostomes and crustaceans. Only the second group occurred in large numbers, and included cirripedes (barnacles) and the less important branchiopods and ostracods. The cirripedes include some genera that are still in existence, for example *Lepas*, which appeared in the Pliocene, and *Scalpellum* and *Balanus* appeared in the Eocene.

Decapods were very important members of the malacostracan group and were represented by macrurans (crayfish and lobsters) and brachyurans (crabs). The genus *Palinurus*, which is common in the Eocene deposits at Bolca in Italy, belongs to the first group. Brachyurans were represented during the Cainozoic Era by a large number of genera, for example *Harpactocarcinus*, *Xanthopsis*, *Palaeocarpilius* and the famous Eocene, *Ranina*.

▼ Section of Eocene nummulitic rock (greatly magnified)

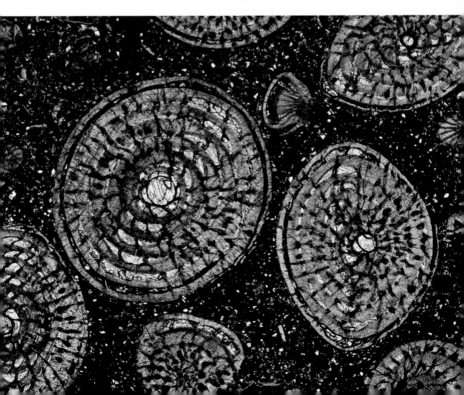

Molluscs were the most widely distributed invertebrate group in Cainozoic times. Chitons and scaphopods, the latter represented by the genus *Dentalium*, were not particularly common. Bivalves were much more important and included many genera that are still in existence, such as *Arca*, *Glycymeris* and *Nucula* in the taxodont group; *Ostrea*, *Spondylus* and *Pecten* in the anisomyarian group; and *Cardium*, *Venus* and *Panopaea* among the eulamellibranchs.

From the beginning of the Eocene onwards there was also a sharp increase in the gastropod (snail) population, which already included almost all the modern genera. Some of the most common genera of the Cainozoic Era were *Patella*, *Trochus*, *Natica*, *Velates*, *Ampullina*, *Turritella*, *Cerithium*, *Strombus*, *Cypraea*, *Murex*, *Nassa* and *Conus*. In the cephalopods the most important nautiloid genera were *Nautilus*, *Cimomia* and *Aturia*. Dibranchiate cephalopods were represented by *Argonauta*, an octopod that is still in existence, and *Beloptera* and *Belosepia*, two decapod sepiadeans.

▼ *Terebratula ampulla*, a Pliocene brachiopod

Astrangia lineata, a colonial Miocene hexacoral ▶

▲ The Pliocene gastropod *Natica tigrina*

▼ One valve of the Pliocene bivalve *Flabellipecten flabellaeformis*

▲ An Eocene crab *Xanthopsis kressenbergensis*

▼ An Eocene crab *Ranina marestiana*

207

▲ Internal moulds of the gastropod *Cerithium*

▲ The Pliocene scaphopod
Dentalium sexangulum

The seas of the Cainozoic Era were inhabited by the same echinoderms that are in existence today. These were crinoids (including the important genus *Pentacrinus*, which was already in existence during the Mesozoic Era), stelleroids, holothuroids and echinoids. The echinoids were represented by a very large number of regular and irregular sea-urchins, some of which were exclusively Cainozoic. Regular echinoids include *Cidaris*, *Phymosoma* and *Echinus*; irregular echinoids include *Conoclypus*, *Scutella*, *Echinanthus* and *Macropneustes* (all of which became extinct between the Miocene and Pliocene periods) and three living forms, *Clypeaster*, *Spatangus* and *Schizaster*. Cainozoic hemichordate fossils are rare.

Moving on to vertebrates, fishes were the largest and most important group of marine vertebrates during the Cainozoic Era.

▲ The Miocene gastropod *Turritella turris*

As in the Mesozoic Era, chondrichthyians (sharks and rays) were
represented by selachians, bathoideans and to a lesser extent by
holocephalians. Chondrichthyan fossils are almost always teeth,
common forms being the selachians *Lamna* and *Charcharadon*,
and the bathoideans *Myliobatis* and *Rhynobatis*, although
complete skeletons are occasionally found, as in the Eocene rocks
at Bolca in Italy.

Osteichthyans (bony fishes), especially actinopterygians, were
much more common. During the Cainozoic Era the
actinopterygian groups Chondrostei and Holostei, which had
been typically freshwater in Mesozoic times, developed marine
forms. Their most important representatives were *Acipenser* and
Pycnodus. Teleosts, however, were the most important of the
bony fishes in Cainozoic seas.

▲ Shell of the Eocene nautiloid *Hercoglossa*

▲ A well-preserved echinoid

The fossils from Bolca indicate how varied the fishes must have been. Alongside genera that are still in existence, such as *Clupea*, *Platax* and *Mene*, there are a great many extinct genera, including *Paranguilla*, *Sparnodus* and *Blochius*.

Marine reptiles, which had been so common during the Mesozoic, dwindled in the Cainozoic and the only survivors were a few chelonians (turtles) and the last eosuchians (crocodile-like lepidosaurians that became extinct at the end of the Eocene).

Three important new groups of vertebrates, all belonging to the mammals, the cetaceans (whales), pinnipeds (seals and walruses), and sirenians (sea-cows), appeared in the seas during the Cainozoic. They left an extensive fossil record, and became as important as marine reptiles had been in the Mesozoic Era. Mammals had become the dominant vertebrate group on dry land, but these three groups show that they had become adapted to the marine environment as well.

◄ *Conoclypus*, an irregular Eocene echinoid

▼ The calcareous encrusting alga *Lithothamnium*

▲ *Exellia velifer* from the Eocene of Bolca, Italy

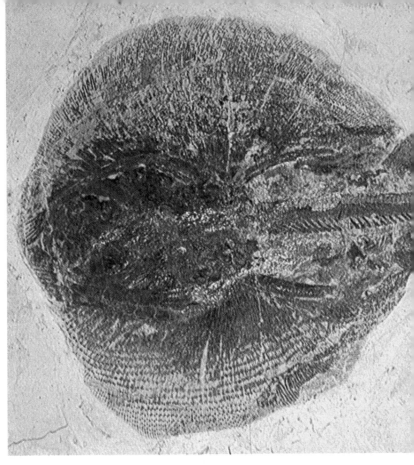

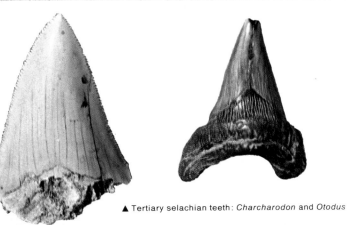

▲ Tertiary selachian teeth: *Charcharodon* and *Otodus*

▲ A ray found at Bolca

▼ *Paranguilla tigrina*, an anguilliform fish from Bolca

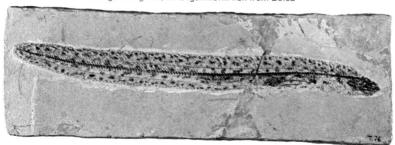

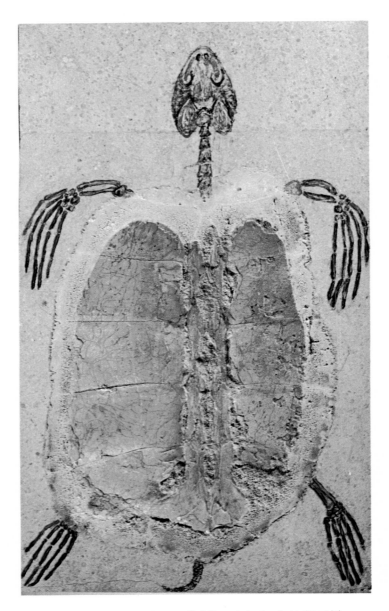

▲ Shell of marine turtle *Neochelys capellinii* (the exterior has been drawn in)

▲ An Eocene marine mammal, *Prototherium veronense*

▼ Leaf of *Zanthoxylon cherpicum*

▲ *Maffeia ceratophylloides*, a plant from the Eocene of Bolca

Life on land

At the dawn of the Cainozoic, life on land changed fairly
dramatically with the disappearance of the last of the large
reptiles. The plants were basically similar to those of the
Cretaceous period, and were characterized by the proliferation of
angiosperms, which had replaced the Bennettitales and
Cycadales flora of the Jurassic period. Conifers flourished
alongside angiosperms. So as early as the beginning of the
Cainozoic Era land plants were of an essentially modern aspect.

There must have been large numbers of insects, judging by how
important flowering plants were in Cainozoic times. The insect
fossil record of the Cainozoic includes some exceptionally well-
preserved specimens, such as those from the Eocene of Bolca,

▲ *Latanites*, a fossil palm from Bolca 219

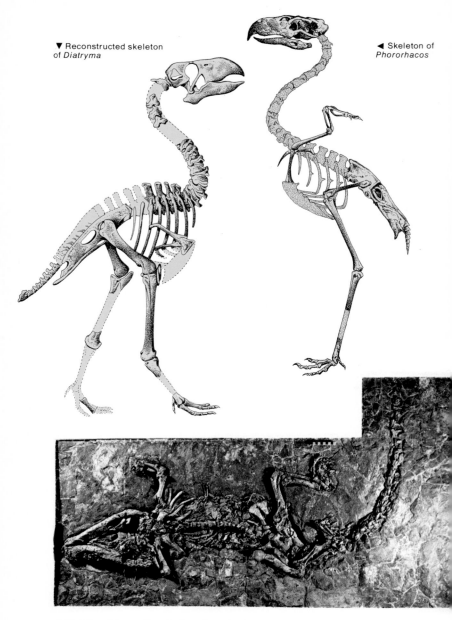

▼ Reconstructed skeleton
of *Diatryma*

◄ Skeleton of
Phororhacos

▲ Skeleton of *Crocodilus vicetinus* (from the Eocene of Bolca)

▲ An insect preserved in Oligocene amber

Italy. In some cases, insects are preserved totally immersed in amber (fossil resin), as for example in the Oligocene of the Baltic and in the Miocene of Sicily.

The most important changes in life on land in the Cainozoic are to be found in the vertebrates. Amphibians, represented by such groups as frogs and salamanders, and reptiles, represented by turtles, lizards, snakes and crocodiles, were much reduced in importance compared with previous eras. Fossils of birds are much more plentiful in Cainozoic rocks than in the Mesozoic. They include birds which were good fliers as well as some which had lost their ability to fly. These birds were ostrich-like in appearance, and include *Diatryma* from the Eocene, which was some two metres high and *Phororhacos* from the Miocene, which was slightly smaller. The skeletons of *Diatryma* and *Phororhacos* are illustrated opposite. Both had well developed limbs, and were evidently good runners, which would have been necessary if they were not to fall prey to carnivores.

▼ hemipteran

▲ dipteran

▲ Insects preserved in Eocene limestones at Bolca

Mammalian domination

It has already been shown that the first mammals evolved from a
therapsid reptile group and appeared during the late Triassic
period, and the history of mammalian evolution can be divided
into three broad phases. The first covers the time when mammals
appeared in the late Triassic period and began to spread during
the Jurassic. All the groups that appeared during these periods
had become extinct by the end of the Jurassic, with the exception
of the pantotheres.

The second phase began when marsupials and placentals
evolved from pantotheres between the end of the Jurassic and the
beginning of the Cretaceous. During the Cretaceous period
marsupials were the dominant mammals and they soon spread
throughout the whole world, evolving many different forms and
specializations.

The third phase started at the beginning of the Cainozoic when
the large reptiles had disappeared. It can only be described as a
'population explosion' and it was to result in these animals
dominating the world. Mammals evolved into some 30 orders,
moving into the sea and the air as the reptiles had done before

them. The placental mammals were commonly better adapted than their marsupial cousins and gradually came to be the dominant forms over many areas of the world. This did not happen in Australia as it had become isolated before placentals were able to migrate there, and marsupials were able to evolve in isolation down to the present day.

Marsupials were also dominant in South America until the two Americas were joined together in the Pliocene by the isthmus of Panama and placentals spread south from North America and are now dominant over the marsupial fauna.

The marsupial skeleton is very different from the placental. The most striking feature is the existence of bones supporting the *marsupium* (the abdominal pouch), although one other mammal group, the monotremes, also has them. Other differences are connected with the skull, marsupials having a smaller brain case than placentals. The back part of the lower jaw also has a characteristic inward-jutting protuberance. The most striking differences in the teeth can be seen in the incisors (marsupials have more incisors and they are larger).

Marsupials adapted to almost every habitat in which mammals lived, and it is interesting to note the many convergent forms between marsupials and placentals, in particular the genus *Thylacosmilus*, which lived in the Pliocene and Pleistocene. It was surprisingly like the carnivorous placental *Smilodon* (the sabre-tooth tiger), not just because of its general appearance and size but because it had enormous sabre-like upper canines. The two carnivores *Borhyaena* (similar to a puma) and *Prothylacinus*, both from the Miocene period of South America, belonged to the same group of polyprotodonts as *Thylacosmilus* and the modern opossum.

There were so many different placentals that it is impossible to discuss them all here, and only those that are palaeontologically important are discussed.

Insectivores (insect-eaters) were probably not very common, but they are evolutionarily very important because primates and carnivores arose from them. Chiroptera (bats), the only flying mammals, appeared in the Palaeocene period, but fossils of them are rare, though there are some large forms, such as *Archaeopteropus* from the Oligocene of northern Italy. Edentates were very widespread and common throughout the Cainozoic, especially on the American continents. Armadillos, pangolins, three-toed sloths and anteaters belong to this group. One of the most important characteristics of this order is that they have very few teeth, or none at all. Their claws are very large, while in some fossil edentates the digital bones of the front limbs were turned

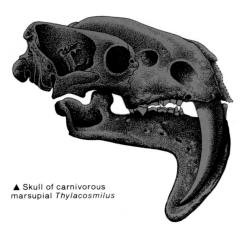

▲ Skull of carnivorous marsupial *Thylacosmilus*

towards the back. Though modern forms are all fairly small, fossil edentates include elephant-sized giants, such as the *Megatherium*, which existed from the Miocene to the Pleistocene periods. The group also includes some animals that are, like armadillos, covered with a thick carapace. Extinct forms, for example the

▼ Reconstruction of the skeleton of *Hyaenodon*

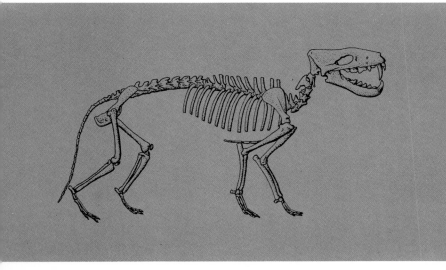

famous *Glyptodon*, which could be up to four metres long, were protected by a single bony plate. (The carapace of living genera, the armadillo for example, which first appeared in the Pliocene period, is composed of a series of separate plates.) *Glyptodon* also had smaller plates protecting its head and tail.

Primates are a very important mammal group, if only because they include Man. The main primate characteristics emerged when the brain case grew progressively larger, the position of the eyes shifted from the side to the front of the head and the hands became suitably shaped for grasping.

Primitive primates lived in the trees, as do most living forms. The habit of using the upper limbs to swing from branch to branch possibly encouraged them to stand upright on two legs, an important characteristic of Man.

The oldest known primates date back to the Palaeocene, and from them such groups as lemurs, tarsiers, monkeys and primitive apes evolved rapidly. The primitive apes gave rise to two groups – the pongids (which includes chimpanzees, gorillas and orang-utans) and hominids (Man and his ancestors). Primitive pongids date back to the Oligocene, and one of the most famous genera is the Miocene *Proconsul*, which was discovered in Africa. The evolution of Man is discussed in more detail in the next chapter.

▼ Reconstruction of the skeleton of the carnivorous marsupial *Prothylacinus*

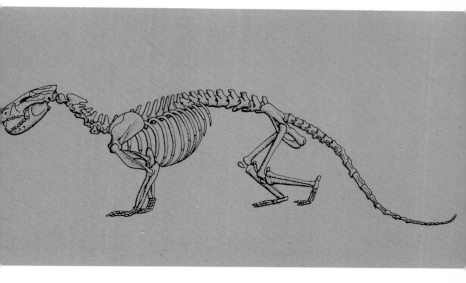

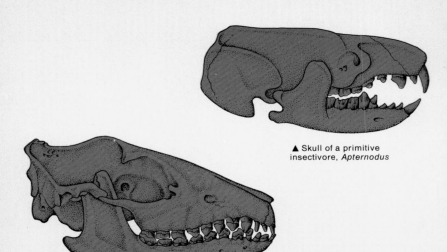

▲ Skull of a primitive insectivore, *Apternodus*

▲ Skull of *Anagale*, another primitive insectivore

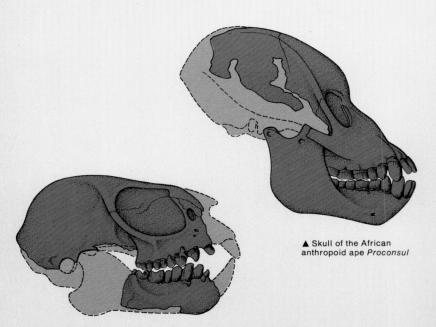

▲ Skull of the African anthropoid ape *Proconsul*

▲ Skull of the Eocene tarsioid primate *Tetonius homunculus*

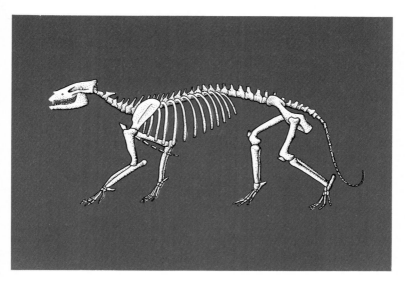

▲ Skeleton of the Eocene mammal *Phenacodus*

Like reptiles, some mammals adapted to life in the sea, and cetaceans (whales) adapted best to this habitat. Cetaceans have a fish-shaped body, very small limbs and propel themselves by moving their large horizontal tail fin. The earliest cetaceans from the mid-Eocene had a full set of teeth like the primitive carnivores – creodonts – from which they had probably evolved. The sperm whale dates from the Miocene period; the dolphin from the Pliocene. Whales were particularly common during the Miocene and Pliocene periods.

Carnivores (meat-eaters) appeared in the Palaeocene, and were predators. Creodonts were the most primitive of the carnivores, but they could probably not move as fast as their modern descendants and did not have retracting claws. The group included the genus *Hyaenodon*, which lived in the late Eocene and Oligocene. The carnivores that evolved from the creodonts are the direct ancestors of forms that are now in existence. Sabre-toothed tigers were a special evolutionary line that evolved between the Oligocene and Pleistocene.

During the Cainozoic some of the most important mammals were the ungulates (mammals with hooves), which existed in large numbers, and had an extensive distribution and great variety of

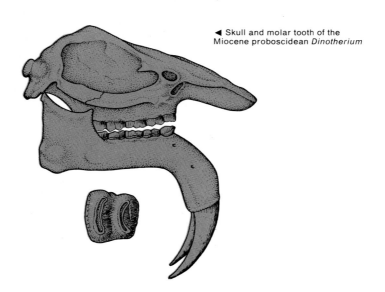

◀ Skull and molar tooth of the Miocene proboscidean *Dinotherium*

▼ Skeleton of *Mastodon*

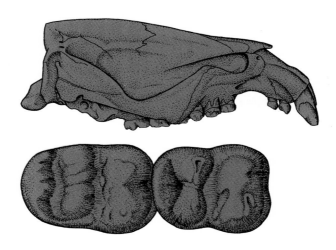

▲ Skull and lower molars of the proboscidean *Moeritherium*

▼ Skull, lower jaw, premolars and molars of the proboscidean *Phiomia*

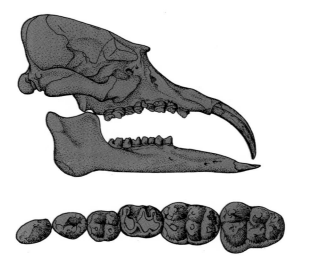

229

forms. Many groups became extinct during the course of the era, but the descendants of others survive as our present-day species. They were all exclusively herbivorous (plant-eating), which we can tell from the characteristics of their teeth. Because herbivores are constantly masticating, their teeth must be able to tolerate a lot of wear. The grinding surface of the molars, therefore, tends to be larger, while the canines, which are essential in carnivores, are much smaller or completely absent (in a few cases the canines have developed into tusks). Other important features of many of these animals are their longer and finer limbs, and a reduction in the size of the ulna and radius in favour of the bones forming the toes. This meant that they were able to run extremely fast.

Primitive ungulates included several groups, now completely extinct, which lived mostly in Europe and the Americas. *Phenacodus* is a typical representative of the condylarths, the most primitive group, which lived during the Eocene. It was the size of a large dog and had features of the creodonts from which the condylarths had evolved. It had highly developed canines,

▼ Skeleton of *Baluchitherium* (the largest land mammal ever) which inhabited Asia in Oligocene and Miocene times

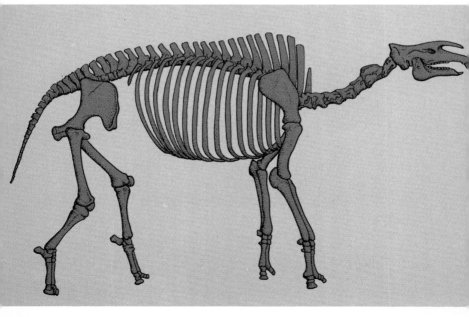

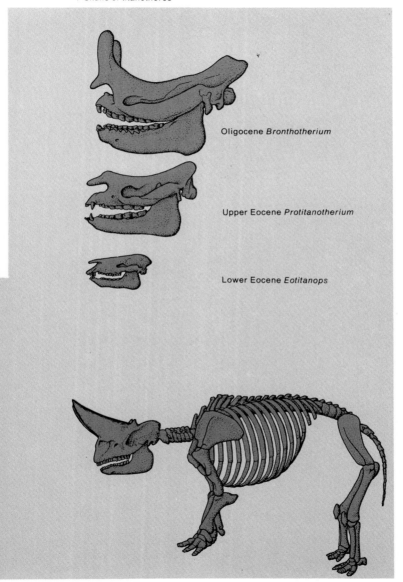

Oligocene *Bronthotherium*

Upper Eocene *Protitanotherium*

Lower Eocene *Eotitanops*

▲ Reconstruction of the skeleton of *Arsinoitherium*

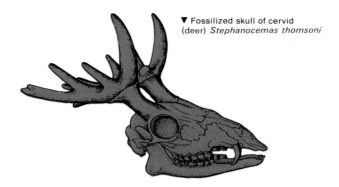

▼ Fossilized skull of cervid (deer) *Stephanocemas thomsoni*

five-toed limbs and a very long tail. *Macrauchenia*, a liptotern of the Pliocene and Pleistocene, looked like a camel. It had an elongated neck, long, three-toed limbs and a kind of small proboscis. The Oligocene *Astrapotherium* was a strange animal. It also had a proboscis, no incisors and large projecting canines.

All other ungulate groups – subungulates, perissodactyls and artiodactyls – evolved from the primitive protoungulates. Subungulates include many different forms, which are characterized either by their highly developed incisors or by their large canines. *Coriphodon* is one of the oldest, from the Palaeocene and Eocene. It was thickset, almost three metres long and had heavy limbs and long, protruding canines. Dinocerates

▼ Reconstruction of the skeleton of *Anthracotherium*

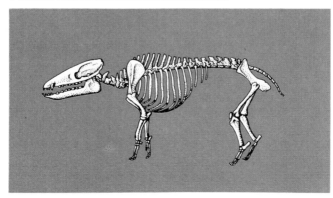

were larger. They were exclusively North American and lived in the early Cainozoic. *Uintatherium*, which was over three and a half metres long, had six short horns on its head and very long backward-pointing upper canines.

Proboscideans (elephants and their allies) are the most important of the subungulate groups. The oldest fossil that has been discovered, from the late Eocene in Egypt, is *Moeritherium*. It is no bigger than a tapir and the typically proboscidean tusks had not yet developed. Generally speaking, as time went by the overall size of proboscideans gradually increased, as did the length of their tusks and trunk. Proboscideans include several distinct evolutionary lines. One of them, via *Stegodon*, evolved into the modern elephant; another, starting with the genus *Phiomia* from the Oligocene, evolved into *Stegomastodon* before becoming extinct in the Pleistocene; mastodons, which also became extinct in the Pleistocene, were yet another line. The Pliocene *Dinotherium*, which had long, lower tusks pointing backwards, belonged to a later line that might be described as aberrant. A skull of this animal is shown on page 228.

Sirenians – subungulates that had adapted to living in coastal waters – deserve a brief mention. The sea-cow and manatee are the only two surviving members. They have a streamlined shape, flippers instead of front limbs and no hind limbs at all. The oldest sirenians, which include *Prototherium* and *Halitherium* date back to the Eocene.

Mention should also be made of *Arsinoitherium*, a strange subungulate genus that lived in the Oligocene period. It was large and heavily built, like a rhinoceros, and had four horns: two small ones on the top of the skull and two larger and stronger ones, pointing forward, on the end of the nose.

Perissodactyls are true ungulates and typically have a smaller number of toes – this can sometimes be just one, as in the equids (horses). Equids, which are now represented by the genus *Equus* (the horse), were the most evolved of the perissodactyl groups. Palaeontologically they are very important because it has been possible to build up a detailed picture of their long evolution. The oldest representative is *Eohippus* from the North American Eocene; his European counterpart is *Hyracotherium*. They were both very alike, being no larger than dogs, and had four functioning toes on their hind legs and three on their front legs. As time went by and the equids evolved via *Mesohippus*, *Miohippus*, *Merychippus* and *Pliohippus* (the direct ancestor of *Equus*), the overall size of the body and skull gradually increased, the limbs became longer and the number of functioning toes decreased (*Pliohippus* stood on the third toe alone). The evolution of the

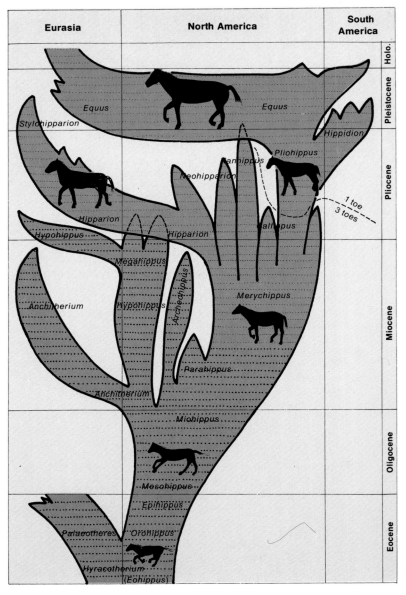

Eurasia	North America	South America		
				Holo.
Equus	*Equus*			Pleistocene
Stylohipparion		*Hippidion*		
	Nannippus *Pliohippus*			Pliocene
Neohipparion		1 toe		
Hipparion		3 toes		
Hypohippus *Hipparion*	*Calippus*			
Megahippus				
Anchitherium *Hypohippus* *Archaeohippus*	*Merychippus*			Miocene
Parahippus				
Anchitherium				
Miohippus				Oligocene
Mesohippus				
Epihippus				
Palaeotheres *Orohippus*				Eocene
Hyracotherium (*Eohippus*)				

▲ Evolution of the horses: leaf-eating genera are distinguished from
more recent herbivorous forms by the heavier dotted lines

horse, from *Hyracotherium* (*Eohippus*) to the present day *Equus*, is shown in the chart on the opposite page.

Titanotheres were large perissodactyls, and were exclusively Eocene and Oligocene. Some, for example *Brontotherium*, stood as high as two and a half metres at the shoulder. Chalicotheres were a very peculiar group, since they were the only perissodactyls that had claws instead of hooves. They lived between the Eocene and Pleistocene and their most representative genus was the Miocene *Moropus*.

Rhinoceratites (rhinoceroses) were very important mammals during the Cainozoic Era. They had appeared in the Eocene and they also gradually increased in size and grew a larger horn. The Oligocene *Baluchitherium*, which stood more than five and a half metres high at the shoulder, is regarded as the largest terrestrial mammal that has ever existed.

Artiodactyls appeared in the Eocene and their modern representatives include cattle, pigs, camels, hippopotami, and deer. One of the commonest fossil genera is the hippopotamus-like *Anthracotherium*, which is often found in European deposits of Oligocene age. A drawing of a reconstruction of the skeleton of *Anthracotherium* can be seen on page 232.

▼ Mandible (lower jaw) of *Anthracotherium*

The Quaternary Period

The Quaternary is the name given to the last two million years of
the Cainozoic Era, and it comprises the Pleistocene and Holocene
epochs. The latter is the one in which we are still living, and it
began about 10,000 years ago, at the end of the last glaciation.
The shortness of the Quaternary period does not make it any less
important than previous periods, and because it is so recent, we
know very much more about it. During this brief period of time
important geological and biological events took place. The most
important geological event was the Ice Age, and probably
the most important biological event was the emergence and
evolution of Man.

The glaciations

During the Pleistocene Ice Age there were several glaciations, interspersed with periods of warmer climate. The glaciations have received different names in different parts of the world – for example Anglian, Wolstonian and Devensian in Britain, and Günz, Mindel, Riss and Würm in the Alps. This is because there is still a good deal of confusion surrounding the correlation of the deposits left by the glaciers.

During the periods of glaciation vast areas of the northern hemisphere and parts of the southern continents, as well as high mountain ranges closer to the equator, were covered by vast ice sheets. Each cold period was followed by a warm one, sometimes warmer than the present climate, sometimes cooler, in which the landscape was recolonized by animals and plants. It is likely that the period in which we are living at present is an interglacial, and in the distant future the ice sheets may well return. The fossils to be found in Quaternary deposits can tell us a good deal about the prevalent climate. For example, in the Mediterranaen region, fossilized or semi-fossilized bivalves and gastropods in marine Pleistocene deposits indicate exactly what the climate was like at specific periods. These climatically important fossils are known as tropical or Arctic 'visitors', depending on whether the organisms now inhabit tropical or Arctic seas. They migrated into the Mediterranean basin when the prevailing climate suited them. The presence of the bivalves *Arctica islandica* and *Mya truncata*, for example, which now inhabit the North Sea, indicates a period of cold climate, while *Conus testudinarius* and *Strombus bubonius*, which now live in tropical seas, denote a period of warm climate.

Similar observations can be made using plants, especially by

▼ Maximum extent of glaciation during the Quaternary Period

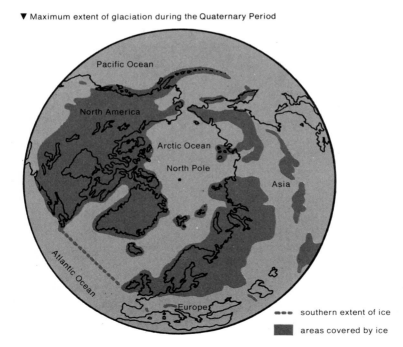

southern extent of ice

areas covered by ice

examining pollen which has been preserved in sediments deposited in lake basins, by rivers, or in caves. Mammals are rather sensitive to changes of climate and so the many mammalian remains that are often found in cave deposits are also useful in the study of climate.

We are still not sure what caused the glaciations, but it might be that certain astronomical phenomena occurred to produce a general cooling of the climate. However it is unlikely that this was the only cause. Indeed, the start of a glacial period was very probably sparked off by a sudden increase in atmospheric precipitation rather than by any extreme cooling of the climate.

Pleistocene vertebrates

The Pleistocene epoch is important as far as the study of vertebrates, particularly mammals, is concerned since it was during this period that the fauna really took on a modern look, although large numbers of mammal species that lived at this time are now extinct, and many were probably hunted by prehistoric

▼ Skeleton of *Glyptodon*

▲ Skeleton of Sicilian dwarf elephants (*Elephas falconeri*):
from the left, calf, female, new-born calf, and a male in the foreground

Man. Mammalian bones left over from meals are often found at the sites of early human settlements.

Proboscideans (elephants) occupy an important place among Pleistocene mammals. At the beginning of the Quaternary they were represented by *Mastodon*, *Stegomastodon* and *Elephas*, and modern elephants have their origins in the last-named. *Elephas meridionalis*, a direct descendant of the Pliocene *Stegodon*, lived during the first Günz glaciation; *Elephas antiquus* and *Elephas trogonterii* appeared during the second glaciation. The African elephant evolved from the first group, while the Indian elephant arose from the second, its direct ancestor being the famous *Elephas primigenius*, which appeared during the penultimate glaciation. In the last interglacial some dwarf elephants appeared on the islands of the Mediterranean, including *Elephas falconeri*, which was less than one metre high. These had branched out from the evolutionary line leading to the African elephant.

The horses of the Pleistocene included *Hipparion*, which became extinct before the end of the period, and *Equus*, which was represented by species, for example *Equus stenonis*, that are now extinct. Carnivores included *Machairodus* and *Smilodon*,

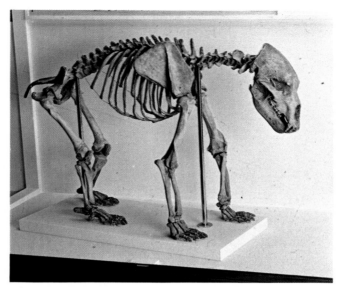

▲ Skeleton of Cave bear *Ursus spelaeus*

▼ Skeleton of the sabre-toothed tiger *Smilodon*

Overleaf: Skeleton of mammoth *Elephas primigenius* ▶

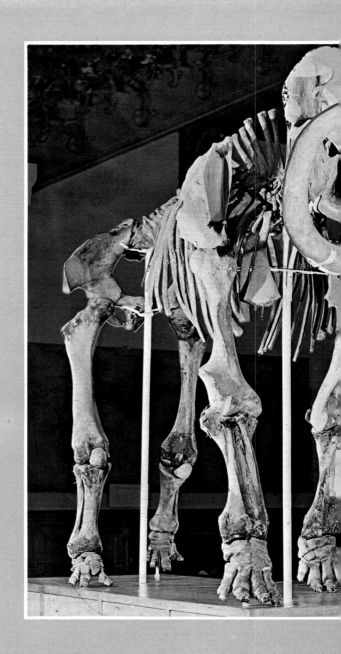

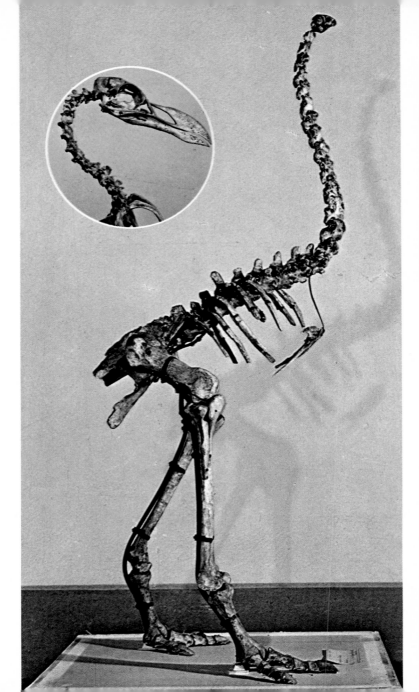

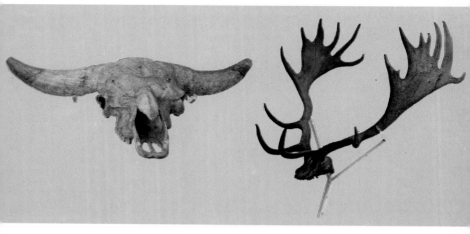

▲ Skull of *Bison priscus*　　　　　　　　▲ Antlers of *Cervus elaphus*

the sabre-toothed tigers. There were also other typical carnivores inhabiting the caves of Europe, among them the cave bear (*Ursus spelaeus*), the cave lion (*Panthera leo spelaea*), and the cave hyena.

The woolly rhinoceros (*Rhinoceros mercki*) and *Hippopotamus amphibius* were almost contemporary with the mammoth. The cervid (deer) family was extremely large and was represented by forms such as *Dicerorhinus*, *Megalceros* (the Irish elk) and a great many *Cervus* species that are now extinct. Elk, roe deer and fallow deer had been living in the forests since the time of the last ice age. The bovid (cow) family included *Leptobos*, typical of the early Pleistocene, and *Bison priscus*.

The Australian and South American Pleistocene has produced many marsupial and edentate remains. Marsupials are represented by such genera as *Didelphis* (opossum) and *Diprotodon* (similar to wombats), while the edentates included the armadillo-like *Glyptodon*.

Birds also left an important fossil record during the Pleistocene period, in particular the remains of some very large running birds, such as *Dinornis*, which inhabited New Zealand in Pleistocene and Holocene times. *Aepyornis*, an enormous ostrich from the Holocene of Madagascar, is more recent. The Pleistocene deposits of Italy and Gibraltar have produced remains of the giant penguin, *Alca impennis*.

◄ Skeleton of extinct running bird *Dinornis maximus*; Inset: skull of *Alca impennis*　　　245

The appearance of Man

We still have very few certain facts about the origin of Man. A
great deal of work is being done in various parts of the world, but
the constant stream of new information always raises new
questions. Indications from recent research are that Man

▼ Evolution of the genus *Homo*

| *Pliopithecus* | *Dryopithecus* | *Ramapithecus* | *Australopithecus* |

appeared somewhat earlier than had been supposed.

Man's exact origin is still not entirely clear and theories about it
often conflict, since it is sometimes difficult to establish the
specific features that separate the first members of the human race
from other man-like primates. The ability to walk upright is an
important feature, and it has been established that one very
primitive group of hominids, the australopithecines, had this
ability (see illustration).

Australopithecus africanus, which is two million years old, is
the oldest known hominid. Excavations being carried out in
Olduvai Gorge in Tanzania have unearthed a sequence of fossil

| Homo erectus | Homo sapiens | Neanderthal Man | Cro-Magnon Man | modern Man |

remains that is extremely important in the study of our primitive ancestors. *Homo habilis*, which is associated with a primitive series of deliberately made pebble tools comes from a level of about 1.85 million years old.

Zinjanthropus, which many people regard as a representative of *Paranthropus*, is slightly younger. Although *Paranthropus* walked upright, it also had extremely primitive characteristics, such as a heavy brow on the forehead. *Paranthropus* seems to have belonged to a parallel evolutionary line that became extinct about 900,000 years ago. The most important species was *Paranthropus robustus*.

The origin of hominids, therefore, seems to be associated with *Australopithecus*. The first *Homo erectus* which is associated with some of the earliest stone tool cultures of the early Palaeolithic (Stone Age) period, was found at another Olduvai level, estimated to be 1.1 million years old. Many remains of these primitive hominids from various parts of the world – *Sinanthropus*, *Atlanthropus* and Heidelberg Man – seem to belong to types closely related to *Homo erectus*. The anatomical features of *Homo erectus* are fairly close to those of modern Man. Apart from their ability to stand upright, important ones are the increased size of the brain case (it was more than 600 cubic centimetres), canines the same size as the other teeth (instead of protruding as in apes), a parabolic palate (not U-shaped as in apes), and a concave rather than flat palatal arch. All these features, plus his ability to use fire and make tools from various materials such as stone, wood and bone, indicate that *Homo erectus*, who is associated with early Palaeolithic (Stone Age) cultures, is the oldest true hominid. Pre-neanderthals (Saccopastore Man and Fontéchevade Man) and true neanderthals, represented by the famous Neanderthal Man, were more advanced members of the same evolutionary series. They are now regarded as primitive types of *Homo sapiens*, responsible for the magnificent cultures of the Middle Palaeolithic period more than 150,000 years ago.

Forty thousand years ago neanderthals were replaced by various less primitive types (such as Cro-Magnon Man), which can be classified as *Homo sapiens*. These types, which are associated with late Palaeolithic and partly Mesolithic cultures, spread throughout the world, leaving behind traces of their existence as well as noteworthy examples of their art. Examples of this include the famous 'Venus' figures (female figurines that were possibly connected with a fertility cult), the numerous artefacts made of carved bone, or the many magnificent cave paintings that have been discovered in several parts of Europe, the most famous being those at Altamira in Spain and Lascaux in France. The way for later prehistoric civilizations had been cleared. In fact when modern Man appeared 10,000 years ago all the most important milestones in the history of human civilization had been reached. The Neolithic (New Stone Age) period saw the earliest pottery and the introduction of agriculture and animal-rearing. Metals were first used at the beginning of the Bronze Age.

At this point prehistory merges into history with the appearance of the magnificent Mesopotamian civilizations of Sumer, Assyria and Babylon, followed by the Egyptian, Cretan and Minoan civilizations of the Mediterranean.

Living fossils

It has been the aim in this book to give some idea of a biological world in constant evolution, so it may appear odd to end by talking about 'living fossils' that seem to have by-passed the law of evolution in which primitive species are constantly disappearing in favour of more modern and more specialized forms. Some organisms have survived almost unchanged for very long periods of time, sometimes for several hundred million years. This is extremely interesting and means that we can have a clearer idea about some of the primitive groups of organisms that once lived on the Earth.

'Living fossils' are much commoner than is generally believed, and they can be found among plants as well as animals. But this section will only deal with the most significant cases and obviously not deal with dubious creatures like the Loch Ness Monster whose existence has not been proved (some people believe it is a plesiosaur or similar animal that somehow managed to survive in a Scottish loch when the other large reptiles became extinct at the end of the Cretaceous).

The most important 'living fossil' plants that should be mentioned are *Ginkgo*, a gymnosperm that appeared in the Jurassic period and is still in existence represented by the species *Ginkgo biloba*, and *Araucaria*, a conifer that appeared in late Cretaceous times and still exists in the Americas. Many other plants with very primitive characteristics have survived, among them *Equisetum* or horsetail (the only living member of the Equisetales family) as well as *Cycas* and *Zania*, two gymnosperms belonging to the cycad group.

▼ *Latimeria chalumnae*, the only living coelacanth species

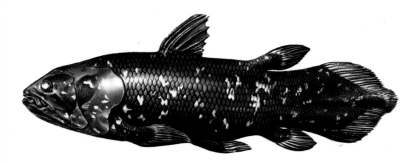

▲ *Ornithorhynchus anatinus*, the duck-billed platypus

The animal kingdom contains many more examples. *Lingula*,
which has already been mentioned, is a primitive brachiopod that
has remained virtually unchanged since Ordovician times and is
still to be found in shallow seas. Molluscs also contain examples,
and the monoplacophorans should be mentioned in particular. It
was thought these organisms had become extinct at the end of the
Devonian period, but in 1952 a monoplacophoran was dredged
from the bottom of the Pacific Ocean from a depth of 1,450
metres. It was extremely like the fossil *Pilina* and was named
Neopilina.

In the arthropod group mention can be made of *Limulus*, or
king-crab, a xiphosuran that has hardly changed since the
beginning of Triassic times, several arachnids – for example the
Silurian scorpion *Palaeophonus nuncius* which closely resembles
the modern scorpion, and a great many insects, in particular cave-

▲ *Araucaria*   ▲ *Ginkgo biloba*

dwelling forms (trogliobionts). These had migrated into caves at the beginning of the Quaternary to escape the advancing ice and there they survived, undergoing anatomical modifications that were absolutely essential for that particular kind of environment, and have remained more or less unchanged since.

The case of the coelacanth *Latimeria* is perhaps the most famous. It is a crossopterygian fish which was thought to have become extinct at the end of the Cretaceous period. In 1939 a large specimen about one and a half metres long was caught in the Mozambique Channel along the coast of South Africa, and closely resembled Cretaceous crossopterygians.

Present day members of the monotreme family, which exist only in Australasia, should be regarded as living mammal fossils. These beaked, egg-laying creatures, such as the duck-billed platypus, are some of the most primitive of all living mammals.

Bibliography

There are many books on the subject of palaeontology, of which a selection is given below.

Origin of Life

Bernal, J. D., *The Origin of Life*. Weidenfeld & Nicolson, London, 1967.

Calvin, M., *Chemical Evolution: Molecular Evolution Towards the Origin of Living Systems on the Earth and Elsewhere*. Clarendon Press, Oxford, 1969.

Eicher, D. L., *Geologic Time*. Prentice/Hall International Inc., London, 1968.

Gilluly, J., Waters, A. C., Woodford, A. O., *Principles of Geology*. Freeman, San Francisco, 1968.

Holmes, A., *Principles of Physical Geology*, 2 vols. Nelson, London, 1965.

Palaeontology and Evolution

Ager, D. V., *Palaeoecology: an Introduction to the Study of How and Where Animals and Plants Lived in the Past*. McGraw-Hill, New York, 1963.

British Museum (Natural History): *British Caenozoic Fossils* ; *British Mesozoic Fossils* ; and *British Palaeozoic Fossils*. London, 1975.

Charig, A., Horsfield, B., *Before the Ark*. BBC Publications, London, 1975.

Colbert, E. H., *Dinosaurs*. New York, 1961.

Colbert, E. H., *The Age of Reptiles*. Norton, New York, 1966.

Colbert, E. H., *Evolution of the Vertebrates*. Wiley, New York, 1969.

de Beer, G., *A Handbook on Evolution*. British Museum (Natural History), London, 1970.

Haldane, J. B. S., *The Causes of Evolution*. Cornell University Press, Ithaca, 1966.

Mayr, E., *Animal Species and Evolution.* Harvard University Press, Cambridge, Mass., 1963.

Moore, R. C. ed., *Treatise on Invertebrate Paleontology.* Geological Society of America and University of Kansas Press (many volumes on separate groups; a few are still to be published).

Moy-Thomas, J. A., *Palaeozoic Fishes.* Second Edition, extensively revised by R. S. Miles. Chapman & Hall, London, 1971.

Olson, E. C., *The Evolution of Life.* The New America Library, Mentor Books, New York, 1965.

Romer, A. S., *Vertebrate Palaeontology.* University of Chicago Press, Chicago, 1966.

Romer, A. S., *Notes and Comments on Vertebrate Palaeontology.* University of Chicago Press, Chicago, 1968.

Romer, A.S., *The Procession of Life.* Weidenfeld & Nicolson, London, 1968.

Schmalhausen, I. I., *The Origin of Terrestrial Vertebrates.* Academic Press, New York, 1968.

Simpson, I. I., *This World of Life: The World of an Evolutionist.* Harcourt, New York, 1961.

Swinton, W. E., *Fossil Birds.* British Museum (Natural History), London, 1965.

Swinton, W.E., *Dinosaurs.* British Museum (Natural History), London, 1974.

Swinton, W.E., *Fossil Amphibians and Reptiles.* British Museum, (Natural History), London, 1973.

Wallace, B., *Adaptation.* Prentice/Hall International Inc., Englewood Cliffs, 1964.

Fossil Man

Le Gras Clarke, W. E., *History of the Primates.* British Museum (Natural History), London, 1970.

Index